THE INVISIBLE
CHALLENGES AND PROSPECTS
FOR AFRICA
THE MISDIAGNOSIS OF AFRICA; VOLUME 1 2018

CAVINE ONYANGO OGUTA

authorHOUSE®

AuthorHouse™ UK
1663 Liberty Drive
Bloomington, IN 47403 USA
www.authorhouse.co.uk
Phone: 0800.197.4150

Published by AuthorHouse 09/19/2018

ISBN: 978-1-5462-9805-2 (sc)
ISBN: 978-1-5462-9804-5 (e)

Print information available on the last page.

Contents

Dedication

This book is a special dedication to my wife and my twin daughters Esther Precious and Elizabeth Baraka.

I am utterly indebted to....

The phenomenally dedicated publishing firm, Author House for their faith in this book project.

My dear wife Rachael for her continued support, encouragement and for being an inexhaustible spring of help and moral support. Her understanding was a sole motivating factor.

Victor Kagot for his immense support towards the project. His thoughts and ideas about the African struggle and what I termed the involvement of the youth in "re-democratization" of the African continent was of paramount insight. I hope to see a literary work on this subject soon.

Finally, with warm hearts to Nancy Birgen, Nelia Mbewe and Sandra Langi my course mates who have been of invaluable support in the concept formulation of this project.

Introduction

Over 55 years if independence and self-rule, African countries continue to suffer from the pre-colonial challenges and confusions which formed the major driving agenda of the first African leaders caucus. The major monsters of hunger, disease, illiteracy and imperialism remain severe nightmares lingering in the minds of every African. Notably, the African dream has been abandoned and the pursuits of which has been kidnapped by a gang of destiny robbers hopping about and filled with 'messiah complex mentality', without direct appointment by the African people. These group of opportunistic and materially possessed misleaders claiming to be leaders of Africa have defiled all odds and continues to enjoy the top cream at the expense of starving population and assigned themselves the power to embezzle and steal resources with an ever increasing level of output; a constant insatiable appetite to get rich by these misleaders. Yet the African people are squarely responsible for every dint they are suffering of. For so many years, Africans have been offered opportunity to elect leadership based on the quality and the content of their brain, but a majority of them prefer to go for other qualities, a factor that has contributed to the mass breeding of ineffective and insensible cadre of misleaders the continent continues to suffer from. The African continent is featured as a wealthy continent with numerous natural resources. The irony remains that the resources from the bellies of Africa are not utilized for the benefit of the African people, despite benefiting many other continents outside Africa. Africans are implored in this book to wake up and reposition themselves in the rightful places before the world. The writer utilizes rare evidences within the African context to narrate the story of the unfortunate perpetual underdevelopment of the African continent, which for the rest of the time has been surviving at the mercies of generosity of other tax payers in most of her sustenance, but even so, management of the generously acquired support is lacking with several accounts of theft and looting of public resources reported every day in the continent. Life gets harder by the day and since the many years, Africans have been moving away into other civilizations to seek "greener pastures" which seem no to be greener anymore. The rest of the world, just like Africa are still feeling the pinch of economic hardships after the major global economic crisis, and service delivery to citizens is taken into focus. Meanwhile, the continued elopement scheme of the African masses is depriving her of her only vital resource it needs to jump start her journey to economic freedom and power. It is only through erection of the effective leadership that the Africa dreams will be secured. The exodus has left Africa with acute shortage of skilled workforce and innovations cannot be at peak. Gainful employment opportunities are limited and communities still suffer from lack of basic services. However, the mere fact that there are no jobs is not seen as an ex cathedral justification to seek for alternative elsewhere. It now remains our own duty to ensure that we create enough employment opportunities. The African youths are taken into special focus and advised on the need to stay in Africa and make their contributions count for the continent. It remains the onus of the African masses to choose which leadership they would wish to have. A fair, just and democratic society or a den of robbers where the poor are used as critical stepping emblem for the rich. Accounts of success stories in the African continent are faintly elucidated with a view to offer the African population a sense of victory. Good leaders from the continent are also mentioned to emphasize the fact that there are no shortages of good men and women in African who are capable of leading Africa into the promised paradise. Electoral management within the African context is viewed with an aim to contextualize major electoral malpractices several African countries have faced since independence. A new dawn for Africa is declared. A new horizon is prophesized to give living hope to Africa and place her among the rest of the continents. But this new phase must have the full involvement of the African people themselves. Even with massive and the unwavering support from the international community, it is imperative that the

African remain clear and fully cognizant to the fact that their own involvement and steadfast commitment in building Africa is the only way to deliver prosperity and success to her population. The generous aid will come as it has come in the past and present. One will pose the question, but for how long shall the huge, massively endowed with natural resources of every unique kind be under the uncertain mercies and will of the rest of the world, who are obviously, just working hard to gain their dignity and success? The Invisible Challenges and Foresights of Africa: *The Paradox of misdiagnosis of Africa* is written at a time when the African continent is experiencing a new dawn. Just recently, about 44 heads of African countries signed an agreement thereby creating the African Continental Free Trade Area (ACFT) which bears the massive potential to transform Africa into a significant economic powerhouse and major contributor on the global scale, and this comes with the express objectives to among others:

Create a single continental market for goods and services, with free movement of business persons and investments, and thus pave the way for accelerating the establishment of the Continental Customs Union and the African customs union.

Expand intra African trade through better harmonization and coordination of trade liberalization and facilitation regimes and instruments across RECs and across Africa in general.

Resolve the challenges of multiple and overlapping memberships and expedite the regional and continental integration processes.

Enhance competitiveness at the industry and enterprise level through exploiting opportunities for scale production, continental market access and better reallocation of resources.

This ground breaking achievement comes about 6 years after the 18th Ordinary Session of the Assembly of Heads of State and Government of the African Union, held in Addis Ababa, Ethiopia in January 2012, adopted the decision. The move is hailed as a precursor of significant consequences but the African leadership is coaxed and implored to work harder to ensure the attainment of the specific objectives of the CFTA. There are no better hopes and dreams available for the African people to achieve the numerous lost dreams, economic growth and political consciousness than the golden opportunity delivered under the CFTA. Equally, imperative attention must be gained in addressing areas of doubts and realistic concerns among the various Africa states, while taking into account the diverse nature of the African continent. As the major problem in Africa is lack of effective leadership, the role of the African population in planting leadership is reviewed and as argued, the Africa people are not off the hook of the blame of poor leadership of the continent, as the duty to elect leaders, to a larger extent, is a civil responsibility, and with most African states claiming a form of democracy, scales are raised on the citizenry to act diligently and vigilantly in instituting political leadership across the continent as a sure antidote to solve the African problems.

Sadly, realities that are of significance remembrance are interrogated. The love and pride of the Africans is no longer in the African continent. The young Africans are constantly on the run to other continents leaving behind low workforce capacity incapable of influencing meaningful growth within the continent. We are confronted with a deluded Africa where wars and constant confrontation within member states is widespread. Many African states are at war with themselves hampering economic stability and political sensibility of the region. These sudden happenings are of significant purpose and must be dealt with conclusively and consciously.

But Africa should have long liberated herself from the colonial oppression and servitude. The tragedy about this is that after imperialistic and pernicious colonialism was shamefully defeated and finally abolished in Africa, there emerged a new form of colonialism by the African themselves under the patronage of the unhappy colonial masters. No sooner had colonialism been abolished than neocolonial project began to take root and frankly speaking, a majority of Africans, still unsure of their own governance, and ill-equipped on the finer details of leadership, played into the game and became worse off dictators and human oppressors. However, inasmuch as we can hold the colonial past as partly responsible for our present economic underdevelopment, we have to ask the question for how long shall we blame the colonial past. But at the same time, is it not ironical that Africa continues to enjoy blaming everybody else, including her own self-elected leaders, while countries that also suffered monumental socio-economic and political schism, torture and slavery from the archaic nature of imperialism and colonialism, are now on top of their economic crest success, and are today displayed, in equal capacity as first class economies? What happened in these nations and how did they raise up from the political obituaries that were written about them to become respected in the face of the world? But then we must also question about what happened to the African dreams, zest and aspirations born long during the struggle for independence and held as the mecca for economic development.

So in our case, we witness what is more than corruption. We have seen what is greater than misappropriation of money. What we are confronted with in Africa is a pure thieving culture that is responsible for our economic wretchedness. Our overall social fabric has been taken into hostage and there remains no sense of guilt or shame on our malpractices, illicit sensual stimulations and negative seductions protracted by greed and selfishness. Sadly, leadership or the lack of it caps the whole basket of shortfalls and remarkable bottlenecks the continent has faced over the decades, and has to be redefined and formulated in a more classical spectrum that manifests into realistic human achievements and development. This is beyond the rhetoric chants and proclamations that have been conversed by the very people who are rightly responsible for the progress of this continent yet they involvement seem to be negating every positive achievement the continent has made in the past. The negative input by a class of unprepared leaders and a citizenry of low reaction even on punitive administration has become critical elements to the failure of the continent. Sadly though, Africans have somehow become accustomed to the tedium of sclerotic authoritarian regimes, often dressed up with democratic frills. There has become a general acceptance among the Africans that leaders must live and acquire luxurious life while their subjects must continue to go hungry at the expense of the leaders. Africans have developed immunity against unfamiliar and unpredictable politics of demagoguery, mischief and deceit. Meanwhile, the continent of Africa continues to be plundered by the very people she elects to preserve and protect her resources.

This puts into my mind an old time series. Back in the days my teachers made us memorize with exactitude and magical prowess the dates and years of the declaration of independence of all African states. Back then Africa had 50 or so nations. The list was long and the independence years varied from one country to another. I mastered the independent day of my country and three of our neighbouring countries and a few West African states notably Ghana. Ghana was of certain interest. My teachers referred to it and the stories of the struggle staged in Ghana for the freedom of the continent were recorded in the history pages we read in books. I loved Ghana's Nkurumah for what I read about him. He was poised as an icon and a true patriotic leader who saw the redemption of the African land. There is a sense in which the story has not changed. Over the years, I came to learn much more about Nkurumah and the more my understanding about him expanded, the more interest I developed for good governance. But I have always asked the question, which liberty did the African nations attain? What form of democracy was coined for the sake of African nations? Was the purpose of this liberty and independence intended in any way to change the livelihood and aspirations of the African people?

The Invisible Challenges and Prospects for Africa: The Misdiagnosis of Africa.

I enjoin myself to the profound wisdom hidden in the masterpiece of a Roman author, Cicero. In those many years, he pinned that:

> "Not to know what has been transacted in the former times is to be always a child. If no use is made of the labours of the past ages, the world must always remain in the infancy of knowledge".

This is why I have constantly sought to understand my environment and to utilize my binocular abilities to look at Africa in three dimensions. The dreams of Africa are well secure and can only be realized when the African accept to work together. The challenges of Africa remain huge and significant several years down the line, and they are still present, in certain cases, more pronounced and worse than the past days. The hope of Africa, has transcended from glim to bright, bright to dark and sometimes has disappeared into thick cloud of hopelessness, yet, the rays of assurance has continued to strike in soothing inclination.

A majority of African states are soon coming to their 60th years since internal self-governance was framed under the auspices of the African people at the helm of power as the main think tanks in managing the affairs of the country. Yet when you think about Africa, you think about diseases, poverty, corruption, illiteracy and name it. While other civilizations are electing leaders who have a form of knowledge on their interests, Africa continues to accommodate in her top power, a breed of leaders who hardly bare any reasonable agenda and sadly still, hardly realize that a leader is not successful until their predecessor succeeds. These old guards cling to power and influence their way, and stick unmoved, as though the foundations of their countries were laid using them as raw materials, and that if they are out of space, then the whole house crumbles. This is indicative that a new crop of leadership has not emerged and, or is continuously suppressed and suffocated by the old guards begging the question "is Africa, moving in the right direction?"

The consequence of these unhealthy and lethargic beliefs has been 'ethnic mobilization of the African masses, rise of untamed corruption and looting of public resources, ravaging poverty among the nations as a result to poor leadership and many more. Our history continues to retain certain names, not for the fair point of good lessons from them but as a scar to the process of free governance. These individuals are in the hook of Messiah complex, and often believe that they were sent from the heavens to rescue their countries from unknown danger, but act least as saviours or Messiahs. The depth of their interests are shocking. Revealed by their exponential growth of wealth, these fellows continue to deprive the African people their rightful share of national heritage by wittingly killing the culture of equitable distribution of resources among the citizenry. Their pride is holed in how much they are valued rather than how much their countries are valued, no wonder, some of them have much wealth, greater than the GDP of the countries they lead. Their desire is to feather their nests and gain prestige using the products meant for the whole population. Unfortunately, the tragedy is that the former colonial powers still instinctively think that they have a divine ex cathedral duty to instruct Africa on what it should do while the Africans leaders on the other hand instinctively belief, ironically, that they have a divine duty to accept what they are told by the former colonial masters. We must as a people realize that Africa needs statesmen and not politicians to take on the mantle of leadership for statesmen will look into the next generation while politicians will always look into the next election. Our politicians are so funny that they will begin watering plants in the rain. A majority of the African leaders, without holding reservation about it, have no sense of touch with the situations they pretend to be handling in their countries.

Not unless Africans stand up and fight from within, the burdens witnessed in the former times will remain constant thorns and source of disparagement in the efforts of true liberation. Leadership in the continent must fight an elaborative corrective measure and this must not be a quick fix, but a dedicated, steady and diligent appraisal pinned on a solid foundation of Africanism. The young African must stand in his rightful places and utilize the influence of their numerical advantage and the prowess of the modern world to deliver on the agendas heavily lying in the hearts of the continent. We must get fast solution to this because this is the only way. We must begin to do what we have to do, and we have no luxury of time to wait any longer in constant despair and lamentations. An opportunity is here with us to salvage Africa and expose her lights to the whole world. This is the only act of revolutionaries: to take visible action at the right time. And there is always no right time than now.

The New Dispensation-A summary of Past Struggles and New Prospects for Africa.

There has not been shortage of people who have talked about leadership in Africa. The topic on governance and leadership has acquired elaborate and articulate discretion from mouths of great African leaders as well as foreign partners from colonial period to the very present, even now we are still discussing about leadership in Africa. I therefore venture into this writing well informed that a number of great minds have elaborated on the African issues far beyond my scope. It did not also escape my mind that this issue has been subjected to discussion in various forums and even in our institutions of learning, it has gained appreciable luxury as a topic among students. I am well informed also that this matter has received articulations from the mouths of our religious leaders and has formed a basic benchmark and premises upon which quality spiritual doctrines have been developed. So the topic or discussion about leadership in Africa is not a novelty of the present age. But why do I want to write about it?

I am adequately informed that way back in his times, a man to whom the progress of Burkina Faso is entitled, Thomas Isidore Noël Sankara had stated, during his pursuits to inspire his people during their revolutionary struggles, that:

> "Our revolution is not a public-speaking tournament. Our revolution is not a battle of fine phrases. Our revolution is not simply for spouting slogans that are no more than signals used by manipulators trying to use them as catchwords, as codewords, as a foil for their

own display. Our revolution is, and should continue to be, the collective effort of revolutionaries to transform reality, to improve the concrete situation of the masses of our country."

Well, I must begin by averring that I do not claim to have the monopoly of wisdom to engage a citizenry, and now a more enthusiastic and well informed society, in the discussion about this topic. However, I am aware that my observations and critical views, some of which I have discussed in this Book, and those of the many heads who have contributed immensely to the subject at hand are vital to continue to inspire a wave of change in the minds of the African societies and cannot be simply set aside since they can afford the privilege of scrutiny as preface upon which this dialogue can be sustained. I therefore utilize this form of communication with a deliberate understanding that it helps in contextualizing some of the dreams and pronouncements about Africa, and particularly on the thematic subjects prefaced by the culmination of African agenda 2063 and its realities in elevating the African continent into equal status among world civilizations. I conclude that these targets should not be mere pronouncements but instead should be well thought-out principles with tangible roots into the consequent change they are meant to spur. We need to actualize them in totality and entirety, in reality and visibly and never on paper work and mere statements in reports. Our population should be able to resonate with these tools that have been founded in the thought that they are suitable means to help Africa realize her potential, and should buy from the idea of making Africa great, if at all these pronouncements are realistic and unique to the African continent. But I hold the view that mere simplifications and decorative figures of speech coupled by a tough talking kleptomaniac breed of misleaders will never solve the African socio-economic and political mishaps, not now not in the future.

Our problems are real: for young Africans continuously seeking jobs in Africa without finding, the problems are real. For Africans going hungry because they can't find food, water and shelter, the problems are real. For Africans in war tormented countries with frequent gunshots, cold blood butchery and disruption of peace, the problems are real. For poor families dying in hospitals because the drugs were stolen or fake ones procured and money meant for the same looted by hungry public monsters and misleaders, the problems are real. For the African patient abandoned in the corridor of wards because there are no more bed spaces in the health facility, not because the facility is oved and out-passes its bed capacity but for the painful reason that there was an allocation to the facility but the gluttonous chief priests presided in allocating the money unto themselves and filed to procure enough beds and health equipment, these problems are real. For Africans dying on the roads because the road construction materials were robbed and substandard roads built instead, we must admit the problems are real. For the energetic African youths whose lives are cut short in the great graveyard of the Mediterranean Sea as they attempt to cross into Europe to seek for jobs and better life, these are hard questions we must interrogate concisely. Why has the Mediterranean been made a graveyard of the African nationals who are seeking to be engaged in Europe and other parts of the world yet African states are termed democratic, independent and sovereign? What does these terms really mean in context?

Africa is a beautiful continent. I must admit that I love Africa and I believe in her so much. It pains me to see how a school of radarless men and women have taken Africa for a ride even at more than jubilee years of her self-rule and governance. I am still pained by the reality that in Africa, not so many of us are committed to the call to make Africa great! I am appalled by the majority of the African men and women who have abandoned the baby Africa soon after its birth and are today found in the flamboyant arms of the luster of Europe, America and now more aggressively in the developed Asian world, not mindful of the African plights and struggles. I am stung by the numbers of the African people who left their countries with the hope to acquire instant jobs in foreign continents but are today classified as immigrants and are now flooded and scattered across the world, as if they are in the process of migration and displacement but even in these status, they can only afford the constant ridicule of apathy and unguarded courtesy. I am ashamed that the African person has had to endure certain mistreatment in other nations not because they were expelled in Africa but because the Africa leaders forgot the top priority that established the African Union and the Pan-Africanism movements early in the days, and instead chose to rule Africa on the hopeless and degenerated promises of yester days. The unacceptable happenings in the world of Africa are what makes one pensive and heart retched about this continent that in my view was most loved during the creation. Indeed as elaborately described, the African countries have generous inalienable shares of natural wealth and resources and better climatic conditions that should be optimized and utilized to bring about change in the livelihood of the African people. We enjoy a rather stable climate and even if not so, we are blessed by riverine resources and massive fertile and arable land that is vital for the promotion of agriculture. I agree with someone who believes that God became a little more generous with this continent and decided to drop a little more of the rare earth and stones that has not been fully exploited and in areas where these are exploited, it is foreign investments in the arena trying hard to raid these resources for the selfish benefit of their own origin while the native naïve owners of the substance is made to believe that the little penny they receive out of the raid is an expression of deep generosity and fairness. When it comes to setting the prices of these valuable stones, Africans have no say despite being the producers but instead have been pushed into the rear edge of the assembly and now are resigned and complaisant as gate keepers! At independence, many African countries assembled their own natural resources and domestic human resources to initiate growth in Africa. While it is of great advancement to take advantage of international corporations and working relations, and this we must continue to do, the modern day scramble to trade with Africa, especially by Brazil, India and China must be put to check. These countries have for a fact, invaded the African continent with massive money, goods, ideas and machinery and are now spotted here and there drilling and mining from every corner of the continent. They have meticulously edged out the conceptual West in the arena of trade and investment, and coming up rapidly, on development aid. No doubt the African nations have certain elements of benefits. But there is need to ensure that qualitatively, we are not losing on the matrices.

We have exchanged our dignity at the altar of poverty with crude dishonesty, greed, unquenchable lust of negative power and greater love for the bad and our problems have been more compounded by our high affinity for the looters and those without vision or our best interest at heart. We have rationalized corruption and turned the fight against corruption and senseless public fund looters by introducing unhealthy legislations that only adds life to the condemned but vilify and condemn to eternity the champions and anti-corruption crusaders. Our tragedy is that we vilify small thieves and glorify chief priests of thieves and lords of corruption by promoting them to higher public offices where they soon acquire immunity against every form of law. We elect the wrong people into public offices but demonize our own agents of change; monstrous public resource looters have been constantly promoted into substantial public offices while at a close range we have rejected honest candidates through humiliation and shame. Our political parties and assemblages, without being diplomatic about it, instead of championing democracy and exercising it in its fullest effect have become small centres of offering instant recognition to individuals based on the depth of their pockets with no regard to how the resources were obtained. These parties have lost the real definition of parties and have resigned into small ethnic trucks used to fuel unnecessary ethnic animosity and intolerance among the people. We have elevated the status of hyenas into chief shepherds of the goats and we become the first to complain when the goats are consumed, yet it is in the nature of hyenas to eat goats, and this we all know but we care less. We have constantly offered a blank cheque to ill-suited candidates and that's why our economy can only be described by romanticist economics as "growing". Yes. It has been a perpetually growing economy yet this growth has no any impact on the lives of the people with early pre-colonial syndromes and aches still our greatest bottlenecks towards economic gravidity. There is a sense in which the situation is similar when one takes a mental tour across the African soil. We have in our countries central banks which have no control over the African currencies and it is here that we have countries with a central bank yet have no currency! It is in Africa where public hospitals have absolute failure of all facilities and equipment yet the private health facilities manned by some rogue health service men and women in the public sector flourish in the negative terms at the mercies of the looted public equipment and facilities and not even the men and women we put in-charge of these hospitals seem to be adequately schooled on their real tasks and finer points of human service. It is here in Africa where top civil servants preside over bankrupt projects or worst still, physical mutilated and absentee projects and use public resources to inaugurate the very non-existent projects, yet the public will gather and celebrate without a second thought. It is here in Africa where the foreign aid we receive from the generosity and sacrificial nature of other civilizations are misused, stolen and are meant for the benefit of a few individuals rather than the whole population but we hardly talk about it, or if we do, it is in murmurs that cannot evoke awareness. We have seen across this continent what must not be mentioned while one is comfortable. We have completely lost focus on the thematic issues that characterized the struggle for independence. It is shameful that the neocolonial error is squarely propelled and fanned under the services and efforts of the Africans themselves. Until we are liberated from the chains of greed, theft of resources shall continue to have a comfortable residence in Africa. Conclusively, it is sure in my view that Africa will never grow her economy on the context of foreign aid, irrespectively of the prevailing terms and conditions it is given. While the donors have always been cajoled to adhere to the principles outlined in the Paris Declaration on Aid Effectiveness, the focus is clear on the African governments, and I challenge them to tackle the rot of corruption, increase internal revenue generation and boost national savings in order to be self-reliant and sustainable economically. Yet I am also of the view that Africa will go nowhere as long as she keeps holding on to foreign aids as the milk cow for her economic success.

We have allowed ourselves to be used as pieces of clay and construction materials for the lucrative houses of the very opulent class yet we ourselves have no houses, not to mention guarantee of food and clothing. We have challenged the supremacy of our creator and instead of worshiping the Creator, we have changed allegiance to the worship of our low voltage tribal war lords and demigods who never lack opportunity of inventing all manner of discourse and disunity. Our discretion of good and bad was long abandoned and today our moral voices cannot speak any moral word, not even to ourselves. We have lost the sense of hope and trust on ourselves but we want to be trusted by other people. We have been synchronized into the kingdom of wolves who are ever eating but never getting satisfied and what we sing are praises to the tribal hypnotized thieves. We are a rare species in the world whose affinity to the wicked self-impost monsters and demagogues is surprisingly high. We have willingly turned ourselves into modern day slavery which is more pernicious than the any history of humanity has witnessed, yet we claim to be better than days before. This is fallacy and stupidity. We have to save ourselves from it. Because in the fullness of time, we shall be consumed by our folly.

Our characters, whether in church or in the pub, secular and religious alike, have remain wanting, and whether the pronouncement that we are 70% Christians for the sake of Kenya and over 45% for the entire African continent hold water or are just utilized in some other contexts or just useful for the mere purpose of publication and decorative narrative perspective is a question we can correlate with our actions is of insignificant reference and as the learned circles will infer, is null and void, at least according to our contexts. We live in a man-eat-man society where what matters most is an individual and his egoism and selfish interests, everyone must fight for himself as in the jungle. At independence, our founders had a great urge and exigency to fully liberate us from the yoke of economic slavery and political servitude. Their agenda was so vivid to each one of them and whether one would take a sensory tour from the Southern part of Africa moving upstairs to the Northern countries, the situation was the same. If you took the direction of the Eastern Africa towards the Western African states, you would find the same mantra as the typical thematic sermon preached by the then leaders. They knew that economic freedom would mean a better Africa free from diseases, malnutrition, poverty, lack of education, and the center piece of the leaders were to deal with these foundational basics in the life of a man. But no sooner had the African champions consolidated their agendas for their countries than there arose the imperialistic regime of new-colonialism in a full fledge of its power and might. This time, the continent was forced to surrender and pay homage to the chiefs of the new administration. The African leaders were disintegrated and often forced into head on collusions against each other courtesy of the master minds of the imperialists, and sooner or later, there were political turmoil across Africa. There was an emergence of dictatorial powers and regimes as a result of the rivalry shepherded by the new colonial chief priests. Bloodshed, coups and assassinations became frequent in the black soil and most of the founding leaders were sooner eliminated and replaced by less imaginative and naïve fellows of the 'astute' colonial masters who began to rule with an iron scepter against their own people. These breed of misleaders fervently and dedicatedly served the monsters and were subservient to them in all ways and deeds. The Organization of African Unity soon became a mere jamboree of near well-doers who had no call for the African leadership and were agenda-less in the plight of the African struggles and pursuits. They allowed the foundational ideals of Africa to be repealed to meaningless expressions of democracy and self-rule. This body become a toothless bulldog which waited for pronouncements to be made at the UN conferences and hurried to ratify them without any significant input from the continent. But we supported them and we still do with a hope that the iridescence moment of Africa will arrive. Sooner we entered into economic vicious circles and our populations, even until presently, are suffering. From the very issues we wanted to free ourselves from under the yoke of colonialism. We are a tragedy by definition, but we are also equally to blame for this inasmuch as we may hold a critical portion of the blame on our distractors. Even as I seek to further this discussion, it is clear that there is not on our side the luxury of blame game because several years ago, Singapore was in the similar states of economic development as the African continent, but after her separation from Malesia, and of course independence, the evidence available to us dispel our curiosity to constantly blame others for our woes. Yet it is not only Singapore. The colonial imperialism and its malevolent were also felt in the Asian countries, some of which have exhibited monumental shifts from dependent economy to self-reliant and stable economies. We must understand the roots of our problems, but in doing so, we only have the choice to utilize these analogies as framework upon which we can fasten our desire for greater development. We must seek to know what happened to countries like Singapore, Kuwait among others, which were lesser in the face of the superior worlds, but currently, stand distinguished among nations, as first choice nations.

As I write this book, I have been prompted to educate myself about Africa. And in doing so I have allowed my mind a little luxury and latitude of growth to ventilate on how the African continent has been perceived by other civilizations. I have ensued on a mental tour throughout the continent and I have a package of the assets delivered by history with me to guide my wonders. It is apparent that Africa is referred to as black continent and this is not only on the fact that the inhabitants of Africa are blacks. Other civilizations have deliberately chosen this term mainly and specifically because of the persistent problems of Africa and the manner in which the Africans have made impacts in exacerbate these problems rather than contributing to their solutions. Africa sadly remains a dark part of the world because there is little light in this arc of the earth, and if there seems to be some light, it is unsustainable, dim and clouded by all manner of chocking that distinguishes the light before it is seen.

But Africa depends on the efforts of her young people to grow her economy. Kailash Satyarthi is credited for this quote and I wish not to paraphrase it:

> "The power of youth is the common wealth for the entire world. The faces of young people are the faces of our past, our present and our future. No segment in the society can match with the power, idealism, enthusiasm and courage of the young people".

But when I look at the desires and long pursuits of our young Africans today, what they put their efforts into, and dedicate much of their time in, I am not persuaded of the capability of the African youth to jet Africa out of her current wows. I see a people who have lost their sense of origin and hovering in the darkness trying to find happiness and constantly skewed and attracted to that which is not African. Which happiness comes in this sad reality? Today our young people are filled with dreams to be in the US, Europe and lately Dubai and other developed civilizations to join the I habitants of these premises in their merry, not understanding the effort and dedication it took for those world class estates to be. How is it possible that our young people want to retire into celebration without any effort and they struggle each day to gain access into US and Europe, yet Africa is a wondering land! How is it possible that the energy and charisma that should build Africa is frequently lost in the Mediterranean Sea when our young people drawn there simply because we have been unable to create an environment for them to actualize their dreams and help Africa to realize her potential? How is it possible that we have only managed to create conflicts among our young people robbing them their unity just for the weak willed rulers to continue ruling?

How is it that when our leaders need engineers and doctors they quickly forget that in our land we have no shortage of qualified individuals, but instead they run to the developed nations to seek treatment and even constructors for their houses? What is the value of the education we have been offered if it cannot help us even in building our own simple bridges and manufacturing furniture, that we must have these procured abroad? Why then is our education proclaimed a universal free education if it is insufficient in the fight against illiteracy, hunger, disease and poverty? Oh, yes, it is free, yes! Free of content and form! No wonder when those misleaders want to have their children in school, they cannot dare enroll them in the free education system, but instead they look for foreign owned centers of business in the name of learning institution to get their sons and daughters equipped as better managers of their ill-gotten wealth, without trying to understand the scope, relevance and goals of such education centers.

We cannot expert foreign based learning centers to be relevant sources of our knowledge well it is so clear that the schemes they use is obviously different from ours. One has to know what impact an education offers to the immediate need of this society. But in any case, we are building our systems in a manner that they will be of benefit to us. We must build our systems in a more reliable and optimistic chances. We have complete learning facilities complete with lecturers and tutors of all kind, and facilities with no limits to courses being offered. But the question that must be asked is that is this education able to transform our countries and enlighten our future. Is this education making us build a self-belief so that we can build countries that we are proud of? Will that education make us build our countries so that we do not seek to leave the continent for other civilizations? Will that education make us have faith in our countries so that we do not have a reason to run away from Africa and participate in a lottery for the almighty green card and Visa into Europe? Will that education us proud so that when an opportunity to go to the United States of America and to the United Kingdom, and to the other part of the world comes, we will come back and contribute to the development of our countries rather than stay abroad and participate in the development of other continents?

Rushing to the western nations or eastern blocks to acquire knowledge for the sake of it is inconsequential if this knowledge cannot find appropriate applications in the local frameworks within Africa. But the sad reality is, while many Chinese and European youths are now moving into Africa, the African youths are running away into Europe, Asia and USA in pursuits of better life. There is undoubtedly something that we are not teaching our youths about Africa; skills to be able to see Africa as a rich avenue, just as the foreign youths are view it. Our young people are not equipped with the skills necessary to help develop Africa to realize her economic agenda. African leaders have contributed immensely, negatively for a fact, to the deteriorated faith in Africa by the Africans. They have mastered how to swindle public resources for personal gains rather than for the common good of everyone. Nothing in the leadership, at least a majority of it, indicates a readiness to deal with issues that are prevalent and pertinent to the continent. No wonder when it comes to taking their families to hospitals, these African misleaders realize that it is suicidal to trust their health with the locally trained doctors, whom they chest thump, to have reserved resources to train. This is a tragedy!

One can only wonder why then do we have leaders who we periodically elect into office, according to what was franchised to us as the practice of democracy! Periodic elections, they say, is a sign of democracy. I have no object but I know it means nothing in Africa. Most African elections have no meaning at all because winners and losers of the said elections are decided anyhow long before the elections are conducted! So the very act of elections is a mockery and a display of the magnitude of insanity in this part of the world. Most African countries invest heavily on elections but the outcome of these elections are choreographed by massive electoral malpractices and open interference by the political class. In most cases, the incumbent have a greater say on all issues related to the elections rendering the entire process an act of insanity if the concept of democracy, free and fairness must be found within the precepts of such elections. Yet election management is presumably done by 'independent' commissions! Well, let us ask ourselves an honest question: in this thing called democracy, are we better off or worse off? One wonders the context to which the term independence is utilized in Africa, especially when it comes to terms of duties and functions of public organizations and bodies. It is unfathomable why election results of no more than a few million voters tend to take more time to count even with consistent massive deployment of election officials who should handle these counting. But that is not significant, in other parts of the world, China notably, it takes a few hours to have full results but don't forget their numbers. African cannot count their own votes! They need help. But even when they finally tally, glaring clerical errors and backward mischief always characterize the whole episode making most elections in Africa no doubt not free and fair. It is sad and deplorable. I submit that there must be free and fair elections conducted under the influence of democratic processes, fully accountable and above reproach. While elections provide opportunities to entrench democracy, it has been demonstrated time and again that they also present real challenges, and in some cases, have been the cause of human mortalities and displacements. I am of the suggestion that there is need for African governments and the international community to prioritize investments in electoral systems across the continent. Electoral justice must be given its preeminence because the lack of it is responsible for the many hiccups we have witnessed across the African content yet it is a major financial cost to our economy. Prudent management and administration of every election is a mandatory prerequisite and we must all venture into ensuring this is attainable, the sooner the better.

Africa had a Dream...But is the Dream still Valid........

I am not an Afro pessimist and neither am I pessimistic about Kenya. What I have chosen is to become a rare observer and a critic of mere academic rhetoric and nicely presented business models that have placed us among the best economies in Africa, with an intention to create a friendly environment for foreign dominance, yet when you get deeper into the villages of Africa, we have no taste of the citations of economic growth. Instead our very own subjects die of uncountable prejudices. When economists look at African countries they generally report our economies as weak. Our GDP has continued to stagnate behind many economies yet our populations have been raising. A population that rising without a positive impact on the GDP is disastrous. On the foregoing, even the attempts by certain low order and busy body classifiers, who presume that the African economy is growing must be shunned as our development cannot be explained away by equating different situations through superficial and childish simplifications. For I seek to ask what is development when our people have no medical care? What is development in the face of rampant corruption and looting of public resources by a few individuals who have elevated themselves into positions of demigods and ethnic chieftains? Why is this called development when it is known so well that the GDP of all the African countries combined is equated to that of France lone? How is this development when 60 years down the line our economy, the over 1 billion Africans, our economy is same size to that of Russia, Finland and Brazil each with have no more that 200 million people? What is the significance of GDP standard, per capita income estimates and other

16

economic indices when our economy is funded through the mercies of the donations from outside our land and heavily reliant on the foreign aid? What is this thing called economic growth when we cannot afford an education system that will help us earnest real socio-economic securities and leverages? What is the role of the international community in helping Africans fight corruption from within, if they have keen interest at utilizing the African confusion to their own advantage? Our problems are real considering that in some of the economies which we have constantly benchmarked our economic growth on are a right antagonist to our real status. We must reject these simplistic comparisons. In Norway for example has in her reserve consolidated funds that that if they were to divide amongst themselves, each Norwegian would receive dissent money sufficient to provide their needs for several surplus years. Over $131bn has been reported to have been made by the Norwegians to share among her citizens through their sovereign wealth fund in 2018. In our situation, even children whose parents are not yet born could be said to have debts on their imaginary accounts! This is a paradox! Partly, this sad and unpredictable snare is due to the constant borrowing spree that a number of African governments have embarked on. It is a borrowing that needs to be tamed otherwise it will be unsustainable in the near future. This dangerous borrowing is crippled by theft of the very resources leaving an ever widening debt that has to be paid anyhow. How then can we sit among the other civilizations and claim equality? Equality on what? Yes we are all human beings but are we equal? Are we children of a lesser god? How can we reject being referred to by most negative terms when all we can do is to rob from the stores of the most vulnerable among us? What happened to us? Africa must begin to interrogate with herself.

We must begin to ask ourselves certain fundamental questions regarding our predicaments. Before in 2000, 191 nations came together under the United Nations Millennium Declaration and ratified what was then baptized as Millennium Development Goals (MDGs). They were 8 and were inter-dependent and were predicated upon health as a fundamental provision and incentive towards economic empowerment. Sadly enough, when 2015 nearly all African countries had not even started implementing any of the eight goals in any serious manner, and no wonder when feedback and progress report time came, there was hardly any sufficient progress reported by the African chiefs. Yet other blocks reported appreciable strides with some, of course, those who had long before 2015 achieved all the possible human development records submitting fresher ideas need of implementing. So they changed the name of the Millennium development goals to Sustainable Development Goals! Sustainable? So we were forced to begin sustaining a development which never existed in the first place and all African nations are today "sustaining" the said development. The question is, is it not extreme poverty, untamed illiteracy, lack of health services, early child mortalities, poor maternal health, increased HIV/AIDS and other diseases, environmental degradation and global raid instead of trade that we are sustaining? Well, the SDGs came on a pillar of 17 goals! Why? Does it means the more we apply an antidote to our wound the bigger it grows? I can't understand why we are now confronted with 17 ideas to sustain development yet we were somehow unable to meet eight ideas in the predecessor arrangement. But to be frank, we still have it wrong right from goal 1 to 17. Why can't these socio-economic pronouncements and fundamentals deliver tangible results?

In order to avoid any misunderstandings: I am not against the MDGs neither do I hold sour appetite against the SDGs. In fact I am of the view that these were and still are significant development ambitions needed for the prosperity of a nation. The only thing that I can never take into my brain to begin considering is the way, time and manner in which these economic ideas were propped up without much thought to the leadership challenges of the African states. No matter how projective and ambitious an idea is, if it lacks a visionary leadership with steadfast focus towards its realization, then its dictates, however brilliant and sustainable they sound, remain foot dust that cannot inspire significant action. The challenge is to develop visionary leadership then follow up by economic agendas. Otherwise we are yet again in a jamboree of confusion while the menace continues at its worst core.

It can only be clear that African have no sensitive economic binoculars. That is the only way to explain the reason why Africa loses every economic deal and instead, continues to receive peanuts from her numerous economic partners she claims to have all over the world. The rise of the mighty economies like China, Brazil and India, the jonnie come lately wealth-hubs in Arab nations and their current intensification of foreign aid distribution in Africa while hacking every potential projects and multi-currency tenders in exchange has certain positive consequences but also bears negative impacts. Although most FDI to Africa still comes from the United States, Western Europe and Japan, the largest increases in FDI to Africa in recent years has come from the Brazil, China and India and now steadfastly, emerging Arab nations. Over the past 20 years, FDI flows from the Brazil, China and India to Africa have increased consistently, only falling slightly in 2009 due to the global economic crisis. While the bulk of the Brazil, China and India FDI to Africa was initially concentrated in South Africa, Egypt and Morocco, they have recently taken a greater interest in intensive investing in other countries across Africa and other developing worlds. While this is positive for Africa since foreign direct investment can be a strong catalyst for economic growth and development, there are serious concerns over the appetite advanced by these economic powerhouses for the continent's natural resources and the negative consequences this explorative in nature-corporations have on the domestic industries. Indeed, Brazil, China, India and the Arab world are already major players in the exploitation of key natural resources in not only Nigeria, Sudan, the Democratic Republic of Congo and Angola, Eastern Africa but in the entire continent and in both land and at the seas and her islands. For example over the last five years, Brazil and China expanded their investments in oil in Angola, Nigeria and Sudan, in mining in Liberia and Mozambique, and in gas in Nigeria. Talks are under boardroom that the newly hatched Kenya's oil will be enrooted to either India or China for processing before being shipped back as a final product from China. These countries are smart and there is no sector of the economy where they are idle and absent-from textile to science and technology, from construction and service provision, they are stinging. They have intensified their investment portfolios in Africa and are working hard to have exclusive market access and advantage. Currently, our own fish markets are characterized by the massive Chinese fish while our own fish farmers are in state of technological scare and appreciation. It does not start and end with the

Chinese fish. And for a possible disclaimer, I am not in any way against open and free space bilateral trades as long as the fidelity of term trade remains tight. But one is prompted to imagine of the fallout of the traditional African industries and service providers at the expense of the carelessness of the African leaders who enter into treaters and all forms of agreements without any form of risk assessments. A number of African companies have been rendered functionless, redundant and useless, and are hit disproportionally by the exclusive entrance of these mighty and unworthy competitors.

Africa's Founder Leaders had a Dream...a Vision and a Hope Altogether, but are these still Valid?

Yet these were the very fundamental factors that Kwame Nkurumah and other founding fathers of Africa fought and tried hard to awaken into the conscious of the African people. Africa began so strongly back then, and in Ghana, there was no doubt that the black people were capable of ruling themselves. Of course several decades later, we need to convince ourselves better. The point is, to put it euphemistically, Africa is certainly capable of self-rule, and yet it seldom features on the lists of favorite nations with best administration, political systems, human rights adherence and so on. Africa has done too little to create a respectable oeuvre in governance issues, and has not made any breakthrough to the powerful positions among the global nations several decades after attainment of self-rule. Can anything good emanate from Africa? Yes. But what is it and when will it come forth?

We are not off the hooks of poverty. More than half of the African population live in abject poverty and degrading conditions. Today they say 47% of Africans live below the dollar, well, it was recently raised to 1.90 US. But whether this is applicable to our situation or not is not the question. What can a dollar or two buy in the current inflated economy that it be used as a reference of poverty index? Well, what I want to derive is that if nearly half of the African people cannot food on daily basis then we are right to be worried about which development we want to sustain. Are we free from hunger? No. On the contrary it has increased among our communities with an unending call by several humanitarian bodies to support the hungry and constant cases of deaths as a result of hunger continue to fill our news headlines. Talk of health, education, gender equality, water, energy, jobs, infrastructural development, water, peace, democracy and the rule of law and so on. What is our index in all these? I know it is below average across Africa with the exception of a few countries whose leaders have proved to be of a different species, but even on such, they have not lasted a time to effect the desirable changes. How shall we kick out illiteracy if our institutions remain understaffed, suffer from inadequate facilities but even if there are staffs and facilities, we cannot trust our own products from such institutions? When our rich men and women, who by all honesty get rich because they have accumulated our own resources and money, fall ill they run away to be treated overseas, when the rich men and women or even their sons and daughters want to go to school, they dream of oversea institutions and since they command the stolen financial muscles, no impediments hold their journey to get oversea education curtesy of our stolen money. When they travel they have personal choppers or can afford to hire private choppers. Meanwhile, we who have constantly loved to see them in such mighty and unshakable positions still travel like Abraham of the Bible did back in the centuries: on donkeys and camels! How will they know that our roads were not built properly and the fact that a road was completed is not an issue, the issue is did it spend rightfully the voter-head it is said it costs and did the materials quoted to have been utilized really get procured and used in the construction in their stated proportions and amounts? How shall we redeem ourselves if we have lost trust in ourselves?

One may wonder why I am so critical about Africa and Kenya in particular. Well, first, in the context of my origin, as a Kenyan I am more concerned about what happens in my country. And my country coexists not in isolation but in an interdependence with the rest of the world, and African nations at the closest. Secondly, Africa is the only continent that has been described to possess more natural resources equitable distributed and enjoys a golden and prestigious position in the globe with no winter or solar seasons, making it ever productive! The fact that some African States import produce from other civilizations is worrying and on this we must find the reason. Thirdly, the massive amount of capitals lost by the African governments due to looting and thieving is more than what is required to elevate her from poverty. Our massive resources have become a preserve for a few high and mighty, who in sheer disregard to principles have arrogated themselves every right of use of our resources. How can we ignore this fact and choose to complain and agonize about our problems? We can never afford another decade of analyzing our problems. We cannot afford the luxury of rationalizing our weaknesses. Time is ripe for us to take definite actions and pull ourselves out of poverty and self-imposed pernicious human sufferings. Time has come that we must ask ourselves the kind of democracy we attained. I know a democracy that presupposes that the people know what they want and therefore take the rightful actions to attain what they want. We must begin to interrogate the premises upon which our democracy was constructed and take corrective measures to restore a democracy that brings with it human dignity and decency. This is the time. We must roll our sleeves and match straight on into the arena of the battle and confront our challenges head on just like David did to Goliath. We must let the characteristic demigods know that while they come through bribes and deceit, we come with the power of our resolution to do that which is right and to end the miseries we have unwillingly been subjected to. I submit that if we are responsible for the bad leadership, we can also be responsible for good leadership. Recently we have been watching the African States where some sense of political hygiene has been seen to be resident, at least in the past records slip on daily basis to retrogressive and undemocratic, autocratic and despotic rule with several accounts of public money looting and the likes. We have witnessed major cities struggle, or in a rash to encounter basic life requirements like water. Of course we shall blame the climatic change as the course of lack of water in these cities not forgetting that in other civilizations, even desert countries have never reported death of human due to lack of water, but instead have excess land produce even to feed other parts of the world? Water bone diseases are a preserve for Africa. Drought effects are a preserve for Africa. Are these not due to anthropological causes? We are the causes of these dramatic climatic changes and we can for sure do something to reduce it. Recently there was cholera outbreak in Lusaka. And this is not the end. There have been reports of avoidable deaths caused on our people. Presently there is water crises in Pretoria. Will it be sorted out for the better? Nairobi is not off the hook of water shortage despite its natural endowment. We can go on and on. But what is the wisdom of citing well known struggles and pitfall about the African continent when it is obvious that only a handful of our cities are in control of the said cities and can provide decent and habitable conditions for the inhabitants? We have an evolution of challenges instead of revolutionary efforts to combat our challenges. Sometimes I wonder why we develop cities and towns and provide progressive titles like the "Millennium city", yet there are unobjectionable absurdity and inconclusive urban development strategies. We must take actions on each of these issues and the earlier we begin the better, for I'd we don't do it, then we shall remain an ever point of refrain in the citation of failure! Africa must begin to educate her people on meaningful and pragmatic disciplines that will rehabilitate and harness her resources in a more positive way for the good of the continent. The Africa elite must be ready to stay on the African soil in order to contribute in the gainful development of the continent. Each one of us must begin to realize our rightful position in the struggle for a better Africa. We are not off the hooks of poverty. More than half of the African population live in abject poverty and degrading conditions. Today they say 47% live below the dollar, well, it was raise to 1.90 US. But whether this is applicable to our situation or not is not the question. What can a dollar or two buy in the current inflated economy that it be used as a reference of poverty index? Well, what I want to derive is that if nearly half of the African people cannot afford a dollar on daily basis then we are right to be worried about which development we want to sustain. Are we free from hunger? No. On the contrary it has increased among our communities with an unending call by several humanitarian bodies to support the hungry and cases of deaths as a result of hunger continue to fill our news sources. Talk of health, education, gender equality, water, energy, jobs, infrastructural development, water, peace, democracy and so on. What is our index on these? The last time I checked, we taking the lead in corruption, poor police service, unemployment, agriculture and name it. How do the rest of the world categorize us? Third world countries. You may say it's not only Africa that third world countries are, but well, tell me which other continent has all its countries under third world class? Ours has become the general global benchmark to describe poverty, hunger, illiteracy poor health and other inhuman ills that progressive humanity should have long concurred in this century. Africa has grown to be an amusing continent despite its expensive deposits of rare earth and minerals. Africa remains the poorest continent in the world despite the heavy grants and donations she receives from the other continents, including human resource capacitation and skills advancement, how come? Do we have success over quality water? Well, I should just talk of water, quality is unimportant when you don't even have something to start with? We have seen an increase in the number of people who cannot afford water and thirst for water has become another cause of death in our communities. This is a tragedy! People die and we lose a vital tool in development; the human capital.

So in essence, our remedy is not with the sprawling, misconceived and messy SDGs that are out of touch with our inherent situations. I think we'd rather forget about them because we will never achieve them anyway by 2030. I am not being a prophet of doom. No. I have seen the pace and the attitude at which most Africans countries and their leaders both in the public from and the private players run their economies. I have looked at the type of leaders the African voters die to elect into public office. I have seen the way the Africa entrepreneur conducts his businesses. Yes. I have interrogated the manner in which the African elites have abandoned Africa to graze in the oversea greener pastures. I have seen how the African worker is being mistreated and several agreements dishonored and abused at the expense of the workers. I have seen the lack of enthusiasm that has gripped the heart of the African youths who are critical factor of development. I have seen how they struggle to gain access to jobs, equal rights and freedom with a constant abuse of their rights. I conclude that it is a long war. Not yet over. Again, I am not a pessimist. I have been in the African content and I understand the modus operandi here so well. Which African governments have put in the implementation plan for these ambitions? Where are the evident signs that they mean well to us? How shall we ever get closer to the goals if all our "public servants" want is to get rich and richer through the very funds allocated to them for development? How shall we surmount the inequality in the distribution of wealth if not even our justice systems are capable of exhibiting equality? How shall we pursue fight against poor health if all we get are fake or expired drugs because a few people charged with ensuring procurement in hospitals conspired to sneak in valueless drugs and siphoned the money to foreign accounts which to my horror, is only known to them? How shall we end malaria as a major killer disease if this is the trend? How shall we end HIV and AIDS if our own medical department struggle to explain how billions of donner funds meant to fight the scourge of HIV was looted? How can we win the fight against corruption if our so called justices and judges are bribed to throw away cases brought to them and in the end set free the accuses without trial? How shall we continue to enjoy the proclamations of a better tomorrow when we inflict pain and suffering among ourselves because our neighbours refused to worship in our tribal shrines and failed to participate in our tribal coronation of "our tribal thief" as our "leader". I am afraid this will not be of any good end and the sooner we get this into our minds the better for us.

The reality that Africa has remained a toddler in the square box for more than sufficient time remains to be accorded its bridal place in the categorization of our challenges. It is sad that we have been out rightly forced to sympathize with certain horrible situations castigated by our illustrious misleaders. And as a people, we have chosen to ridicule such misleaders without the proper intent to change the quo. We ridicule their actions of ignominious chagrin but continue to elect them into public offices to serve. We are abhorred by their greed and creed to selfishness but we rather have them as demigods. A majority of us, without being sarcastic, have been reduced into sycophantic sympathizers and are characterized by the absence of wisdom in their choices. We do not uphold the consequences of positive leadership because we have never had a chance with positive leaders. The beauty of good governance is not in or lips neither is it our aspiration. But can we afford to continue with such treacherous uncivility of character?

Responding to a Call for a New Broom that Promises to Sweep our House Clean...

We must ensure that we engage suitable individuals in our midst with the responsibility of leadership and governance. These individuals must not be permitted to metamorphosis into earthly gods who would seek to ruler over us until their graves pull them in. They must be men and women of wisdom who understand the plight we go through and who have a rare sense of integrity worthy of a leader. They must be exemplary through conduct and deeds and prove that indeed Africa was created great, not by a lesser God but on the contrary, a more generous and diverse God who sees all of us as equal regardless of which tribe, race or region we come from. They must be unique people who will help us realize our potential in all spheres of life and will be ready to sacrifice self on the altar of morality just to create a better society. They must be those who will inspire us even when we are on our last breathe and encourage us to move on with a constant promise of unwavering support. Yes, they must be the great among us who have dedicated themselves and struggled to earn their wealth through verifiable and just mechanisms and not individuals who betray our trust for the sake of senseless accumulation of our hard earned resources. They must be, by basis of consistent evidence, accountable and trustworthy because leadership without accountability equals mis-leadership. These are the people who we must allow to climb onto our portfolio of leadership and grant the fair side of the dice to prefect our development.

I submit that there is no shortage of good leaders in Africa and over the past few decades, we have witnessed some fresh breeds of individuals sprout at different spots in the soil of Africa and their positive and fulfilling impacts have been felt. The land of Mauritius has seen these fresh breeds and is now classified among the top list of best governed countries in Africa. But I must clarify out that I am not a supporter of classification systems and criteria employed by failed regimes and organizations with sinister motives, mostly franchised and thumped by foreign arrangement. I am basing my views on evidential strides attained over the past periods of leadership and how that has impacted on the lives of the common man in the country. Botswana's immediate former President Ian Seretse Khama was seen to be performing reasonably fair until his recent resignation on the 31st March 2018, and whether one chooses to believe it or not, there is a new wine in the pot of Botswana. I am aware that he attracted positive criticism over corruption allegations and his style of leadership, and it is not outside my scope that his track record with corruption was commendable and positively influential to the rest of Africa. I hope he remembered to groom a team and that his successor president Mokgweetsi Masisi who was sworn in on Sunday April 1 has greater skills in the win making industry, and will continue to track the paths of development. We can cite several priorities for Botswana, including job creation for her youths and overdependence on diamond mining that has to be addressed, to slow but recently picking up economic growth. But since a pace has been set, the prospects remains high for Botswana. Tanzanian's top man John Pombe Magufuli is a hardworking man and today, whether one agrees or not, there is a new sense into which Tanzania is moving, and doing so steadfastly and very fast. Someone once told me that in spite of the records, Magufuli is trembling on democracy and several other complaints. Well, I do not share that view at all and I will elaborate my thoughts shortly. I was remember I had a long discussion with a friend from Tanzania and all our thoughts were uniquely filled with complementary phrases to Magufuli. He described to me what in his view, were the greatest achievements of the president and I could only agree with him entirely.

Throughout this short interaction with my Tanzanian friend, we kept reminding ourselves of how ugly Tanzania was quickly gravitating to just years before Magufuli came to focus and why we thought Magufuli should be present longer to incubate some sanity in the house. I also presented my thoughts to him and in our conclusion, Magufuli was doing above average. Over the past years, we have witnessed Mali's President, Ibrahim Boubacar Keïta, Cameroon's Paul Biya and Burkina Faso's Blaise Compaoré showing impressive score cards. It is not vanished in my memory that not so long ago, we had leaders like Nelson Mandela, a man whose Pan-Africanist credentials are heavier than my writings, Julias Nyerere, the Tanzania founding president, Patricia Emery Lumumba, Thomas Isidore Noël Sankara of Burkina Faso whose leadership set an electrifying example across Africa, the Osagyefo Kwame Nkurumah, Kenneth Kaunda, Ahmed Ben Bella, Robert Sobukwe, Albert Luthuli, Nnamdi Azikiwe, Abner Nasser, Amilcar Cabral, Sekou Toure and many other founding African icons who demonstrated that leadership was only defined by the dedication to constantly ameliorate the living conditions of your people while holding the highest levels of accountability and undoubted integrity standards.

It remains my hope that the achievements of the present leaders will remain valid and not soiled by competing selfish interests and degeneration into political demagogues, something that was unique and common in a majority of the first assembly of African leaders, and that the influence of developed nations and development partners in Africa will be to the extent of helping Africa improve her situation for the betterment of her people. What Africa needs is not a demigods who will demand reference from people but visionary and intelligent servants who will lead through words and deeds in the realization of full freedom. No leadership position should be seen to be a preserve for a certain people. African leaders must learn when to exit the scene and not to cling unto power against the interest of the public. It is often said that when a bird stays for too long on top of the tree, it attract stones, and of a recent case Mugabe did this in Zimbabwe-now he is out through the very first free and fair *coup-d'etat* in Africa. African nations need people who will put aside the allure and luster of power and willing to demonstrate to the rest the value of hard work, respect to the existing commonly accepted rules of the land and the way to fight our greatest economic enemies. Such are the ancestral disappointments that we must avoid at all costs. The Burundian president has of the most recent case been a testament that Africa has new breed of leaders who are beginning to have substance in their brains and understand that getting opportunity to serve does not mean that there are no other who could serve. Pierre Nkurunziza had already registered a negative page with records of history over his three year rule, and particularly, his controversial victory in 2015. But his recent decry not to vie for re-election after the end of his current tenure in 2020 is a move towards the right direction. Earlier, his championing a constitutional change that has seen the country extend the constitutional limits for the presidency, was seen as, it is usually the norm, a move to plant himself forever at the realms of power. His administration has been seen to be degenerating into a politico-religious mysticism and one will observe that there is a growing cult around his the presidency. Such are the absurdity the Africans people have found themselves in. While Nkurunziza believes that his leadership descended from God and that God in His divine will set him apart to rule over his people, the extent at which this belief took a majority of his fanatic sycophants is unfathomable. Respecting term limits is vital to the progression of democratic dispensation in Africa. Those who choose to stay put as it has happened with some must be strongly condemned against this vice.

While it is important to acknowledge and celebrate that Africa has witnessed the emergence of leaders with a vision to move Africa forward, beyond the dreams of independence, the bottleneck has been a huge bunch of leaders ignore their role in shaping the next generation of leaders who will take over after them. A majority of the leaders have no agenda for their nations and neither do they understand the course of their nations nor the plight of their subjects. Currently, a number of African leader are in a rash to extension of term limits or even an abolition of the same. Their refusal to leave power at the appropriate time is intoxicating and must be stopped. We must know that the individual holders of office are merely cogs in the wheel whose presence are utilized and remain replaceable for the wheel to keep moving even after they are won out. In order to allow institutions to grow, in order to allow African nations to achieve their absolute and unique potentials, the majestic and near monarchical occupation of power by certain individuals must be checked so that public offices are not necessarily turned into personal rooms where the occupant hold the power to invite and expel, while on a loose end to personalize public utilities.

Julias Nyerere, Nelson Mandela, Sir Seretse Khama, Festus Mogae and Quett Ketumile Joni Masire were exemplified African leaders who served Africa in her best interests and with exuberant of a latter day missionary demonstrated that holding leadership position is not supposed to be mistaken for a grand lottery win but is an opportunity of service to the people. These are a few testaments that demonstrate that Africans had a vision before this vision was rudely adulterated and smashed by the weakly equipped crop of misleaders who popped up after the first generation of leaders. They demonstrated that leadership is a means through which a people can chat their direction and by utilizing the powers embedded in their strengths, prop up into the highest of potentials. When fully agitated, the people ought to rise above their necks and begin to irritate leaders to invoke their proactive forms and begin to take the lead in excellence. Such requires a people who will stand at the top of the rooftops like John the Baptist did and remind elected leaders that they are just but servants who must act efficiently and diligently in acquiring services for the common good of their subjects. These crew understood the leapfrog theory so vividly that Nkurumah, soon after ascending to power, began to make impressive economic undertones that has since place his country Ghana ahead of many African countries. He took to himself the reunification of the nations because unity in diversity was an incredible and inevitable mix into the flavor matrix of the socioeconomic and political arrangement. Today, as already discussed herein, Africa stands a better chance to display best leaders who have begun to put the African house in order. Mentioning Ellen Johnson Sirleaf of Liberia, Ian Khama of Botswana, Ameenah Gurib of Mauritius, Adama Barrow of the Gambia, Danny Faure of the Seychelles, Hage Geingob of Namibia, Roc Marc Christian Kabore of Burkina Faso, John Magufuli of Tanzania, Paul Kagame of Rwanda and Nana Akufo Addo of Ghana is a positive demonstration that a paradigm shift is occurring in Africa's leadership. I can begin to have a feeling that Africa will soon be a topic of discussion with regards to good governance when leaders are elected on the basis of their willingness to steer their countries along the trajectory of development. We must therefore offer uninterrupted opportunities to figures such as these to be in charge of our development. Emergence of perpetual thieves, dream killers and bearers of bad fortune must be exterminated and denied the opportunity to rise in our midst. We must elect accountable and visionary men and women as our leaders.

We did not inherit a hereditary form of governance where leadership is a preserve for a certain material or breed of individuals and when they are not leaders, then there is, in their view, a crises of leadership. Our ancestors fought for an inclusive form of governance where everyone was to be treated equal and had the equal chance of leading as long as they bore the agenda that drove the minds of the people and were at the best interests of the people. This is what we must allow ourselves to exercise without prejudice. I am happy that when people will rise to their duty of preserving leadership, ineffective political shenanigans will have no room to hide and will be forced to flee for safety elsewhere. A moment of political upheavals is coming for the un-sagacious African leaders and it is time they took note. The old guard who for a long time have held the view that their DNA forms what leadership ought to be and on their terms the same must be interpreted must be prepared to spend longer times of emotional trauma as a result of what will transpire in the coming seasons. Dynasties that have taken Africans into hostage and long periods of self-slavery will scramble.

We cannot be under the tutelage of the pernicious slavery castrated by the latter day colonial masters any longer. It is time we took off the clothing of slavery and wore new regalia in readiness for the battle to salvage our continent from a continuous bitterness of servitude and disparage by other civilizations. Africans must rise up and realize that the world will show respect to Africa if they become fit in raising solutions to current world problems and not by being problems to be solved. We cannot afford to perpetually be seen as lesser people who have no form of direction and make no contribution to the course of humanity but a scar in the conscious of humanity. It is high time the true African political class made sense of their politics and come to the battle field of human civilization to fight tooth and nail to deliver Africa from the fangs and claws of dangerous monsters crippling onward in the form of neo-colonization and the conception that Africans can only fit to serve as hewers of wood and drawers of water at the building site must be challenged when our elites rise up to the occasion and begin to take informed decisions on how best Africa must be managed. The hostage inclination to former colonial warlords must be interrogated passionately in order to dissuade the interest of people who are falling into intimacy with short term presents offered to African states at global assemblies and by effect clear the vague in their eyes to be able to look up properly at the resource Africa holds in her belly. When we realize the value of our resources, we shall begin to create manufacturing hubs so that we don't engage in the exchange of raw goods for their finished products which come back at expensive prices.

Yet the African individual must also exhibit a radical change of attitude and be more willing to participate in the developmental efforts to rebuild Africa and increase their interest in doing that which is good and right. We must be constantly fed by the wisdom of Mahatma Gandhi when he said that one must not lose faith in humanity because humanity is an ocean; if a few drops of the ocean are dirty, the ocean does not become dirty. We cannot lose hope in ourselves. But I still hold the view that leadership by itself is not the sole solution to our challenges but is an indispensable recipe in the attainment of absolute freedom. By effect we must integrate into good leadership responsible citizenry. We must decorate it with open mindedness and change of attitude. We must exhibit its effects by participating in good governance. When we are offered an opportunity to elect leaders, our priorities must change and focus on those who will do what it takes to inspire development and roll our serious campaigns on how we can do our things better. We must not allow greed and other negative attributes that have overruled our decisions in the past to take pivotal points in this war. We must be willing to elect leaders, not on the basis of their ethnic extractions or depth of their pockets, but in the mere basis of the content of their brains and their ability to constructively engage us in the efforts to develop our nation. Our fight must be against the vices our communities have suffered and not on mere ethnic based antagonists and cheap political subservience.

Understanding the Role of the African Youth and its Fulfilment.

The African youth must come out fervently to resist the temptation of sycophancy and senseless dependence on negative politics and political warlords whose primary goal is to use the confusion of the young people as a suitable platform to ascend into greater positions at the detriment of the society, and begin to perform the role of a cornerstone. Our societies must begin to embrace the full meaning of peace and enjoy the full flavor that comes with it, not in the mere consequences of the absence of war but on the account of our ability to create an environment that hatches equality among us and where there is fair administration of justice. We must develop a merit based society where we all have rights and freedoms, not at the declaration and prerogatives of certain individuals, but as an inalienable component of our systems.

But it does not stop there. The prospects we anticipate will never arrive on a silver platter as did the missionaries. It has to be delivered through the application of effort in the things that require effort. We must be present in the fields doing our agriculture in a more elaborative and sophisticated manners we have learnt from other civilizations. We must be available in our places of work delivering quality services to our people and not subjecting our own people into cheap lordship syndromes. We must be present and alive at our cottage industries to give credit to our skills and improve our own sectors. Our young people must be present in the financial arena to study how economies are developed and utilize these knowledge for the benefit of the society. We must allow our thoughts to be engaged in critical disciplines that will help us be self-reliant and productive as a people and not to suffer from a consistent paralysis of analysis by other civilizations and general characterization as aid seekers. This is the season to display and concur by the sweat of our braw. The categorization of the African personalities into two sets of opposing forces must be challenged. It is widely accepted and when you take a look at the African society, you will immediately notice that there are two sets of personalities present: those who are typical of their hard work but make no living out of it and those who do very little or best said literally noting but live lavishly and stylishly at the expense of the rest of the society. What is amazing and difficult to comprehend is that the latter category comprises also and mainly of the leadership bracket! The former set does not have contact with the elites, or there may be it is mainly for election purposes and soon after the election a wall is built between these sets. We must be alive at our duties to make an extra coin through the sweat of our brow and not simple diabolic machinations presently disposed to our young people through lottery games, gambling and betting that today has become a center of engagement as well as a recipe for death to some young people who sloth the idea of hardwork, but wish to enjoy the meaning of life with all its prestige and flavor. We cannot afford to develop our economy through such schemes and those who want to be lethargic and rip from where they did not sow must be alive to the fact that gone are the days when manner fell from heaven, and that in the present day, you must be willing to roll up your sleeves, take on your hoe and till the garden to eat tomorrow. We must never allow the Garden of Eden syndrome and the Rich Subaltern Mindset to be present in our minds because never again will we eat without making an effort, and far be it from us if we are hooked to the thought that it is only by serving other civilizations that we shall emerge economically viable as a continent. We must offer ourselves to meaningful and productive labor. We must hold true to our values and morals that direct us that we must dispel disunity amongst us, we must remain in our right moral judgment and never allow prejudice and inconsequential appetite of other civilizations to dissolve us. We must chat the way forward for our continent together as a people, and only invite other civilization to be present as witnesses that Africa can govern herself without having to be directed by laws and regulations franchised in other continents.

We must work in the awareness of modern technology and be the first to embrace fundamental innovations in order to increase our production. In agriculture we must allow serious agrarian revolution to take shape. In the industrial sector, we cannot afford to miss out in modern industrial revolution and in education, technology must be a well grasped subject. The education system we implement should be able to teach us to apply more pragmatic means to transform knowledge into real development. It must not be contextualized on the mere basis of the strength of academic mastery without functional output but on the basis of its ability and capacity to be practically applied in the problem solving models. Our agriculture must be given the due diligence it deserves to grow from its current agrarian form into mechanized agriculture that incorporates sufficient elements of sustainability as well as technology. Our education must change to allow us be better managers of our resources rather than being sustainers of failed forms of attempted natural conservation principles. We must be able to interrogate the factors that make our society healthy and invest in them. This calls for real participation in the efforts. We need to have an economy that grows. Not a compilation of what is called nominal GDP that does not reflect the actual situations on the ground. A low level farmer in the village should appreciate a rise in per capita income just as one living in town does. As it is today, the epistle of per capita increment means nothing to a villager who sleeps without food not once but several times a week. The mere pronouncement of growth in our economy adds to conviction to a woman who faces death of her child because she can't afford to take her to the hospital. There must be a balance on measuring real economic values and evaluating peoples' aspirations and possibilities. An increased rise in public debt and constantly skyrocketing inflation rates never mean well to an economy, and especially if the return on investment is on the decline. So we have to change our economic models and put in place effective, factual tools to rate our development. A development in which we all participate in making since we must all pull together in one direction. The continue portrait of the African person as a beggar by the Beautiful Gate must come to an end and it will only end if Africa begins to utilize effectively every single individual from Africa and not to allow them to be scattered across and about the world. The mind and attitude that drives the African man into slavery several decades after it was officially abolished is a kind incapability that requires sophisticated forensic studies and diagnosis.

Not so long ago, in the 1990s to be elaborative, it was widely accepted, and of course many writers and economists then also had similar input, that the heavily-indebted countries, particularly in Sub-Saharan Africa require relief initiatives beyond mere rescheduling to have a turn-around in their economic performance and fight against poverty. Well, this was the guiding principle to the donors and in the late 1990s, courtesy of economic review articles, this understand appeared to have stirred the international community to consider broader and faster external relieve through a complex debt initiative policy. I do not hold something huge against this initiative. Yes. Through it, many African countries began to stir around their understanding of economic development even if this meant literally nothing to them, and before long, some fruits were presentable. But this debt issue has been utilized beyond its limit. I will consider, in this presentation the case of two classical nations, today in the first class, but at similar times as Africa, were in lower standards as compared to several African nations. Their stories is what makes me think that this debt thing is killing our energy before it is spent. IMF in 2001 while using what I have termed romantic economic theorem and axioms, prophesied that Kenya would reach her sustainable levels of debt without special help from the "pernicious debt scheme". Presently, our external debts are so huge and widespread that it would be said that every unborn Kenyan, for instance, already has a huge share of this debt, if everyone was to pay the debt upon birth. Today we are indebted to China and if things are not changed sooner, we shall become a second significant property under the mainstream chiefdom-hood of the Chinese. But this does not keep the itching hands from seeking more. What pains the most is the manner in which these borrowings are expanded: into luxuries and prestige by a few unsatisfied fellows whose grave and yearn for more is certainly insatiable. Our Central banks have purportedly reported tight growth margins and are perpetually deluded that by periodically injecting currencies into the economy, there is a rise in the general growth. It has become a voodoo system of management! Since 2001, our GDP, the 1.6 billion of us, has been dwindling somewhere in the neighborhood of "weak" and "better than" but when you investigate what it is better than, you are reminded of the war torn nations of Syria and Cuba. With only a projection of 3.5% GDP in 2018, African countries have a lot to do in order to remain active in the global economic scheme. It is less the GDP estimates of France for the same year. It remains sad that Africa combined, continues to lag behind many European countries, which are much smaller and with less human resource power. Sadly, we are told that the rates of borrowing are sustainable. The question these idlers avoid like the plague is, on whose back and sweat is it sustainable? Every government on ill-advised foreign debt borrowing spree must stop to think about the future of their countries long after them. When a country depends on nothing but borrowing while corruption is not checked, the value for the money borrowed is lost and the entire nation is subjected to long term economic instability.

We have been paying more funds than we receive because no sooner than the funds are realized by the creditor, we mysteriously 'disappears' never to reach the national coffers. This, as our modern day economists will always tell us, reduces the domestic resources available for our development. African countries export their primary raw products while import the finished products out of them but even this export is getting smaller by the day. Our industries are old fashioned and heavily human labour oriented and we spent much in labour weighing into the marginal dividends. Other than labour, high electricity costs impedes our desire to develop. Aside from the external debt, it would be interesting to understand that Kenya's internal/domestic debt is equally proportional. This is why I believe that we must get new minds in the economic planner table for Kenya to blow fresh thoughts in tandem with the current revolving economic world. The pace at which the world is moving at must be matched by certain specialties of thoughts that can innovate new and better schemes to solve our economic riddle, far much better that the current understanding that thinks that by the government reducing the number of public servants, an economy can grow. What we need are radical and eruptive proposals that will touch the moral fabric, inject calculated doses of antidotes of insomnia to lethargic minds, and challenge the powers of the economic elites who are in the business of consistent wealth accumulation and deprivation of economic freedoms. These are the cartels in the monopolistic assembly of involute tenderpreneurs. They are credited to be running the economy of the nation but their means of wealth accumulation is stripping the weak of every value. They claim the political power, but the people they pretend to be leading die often of retrogressive and backward-day calamities including water bone diseases. They command and demand salutes and fancy names and titles without responsibility and accountability. These are the abhorrent acts and deeds we must rid of our societies in order to periscope our destiny in clearer and unperturbed frequencies. And the gap between the rich and the poor continues to grow exponentially. I can bet all my balls that the situation is the same when one goes from South Africa to Cairo, and return through the Sub-Saharan region of Africa.

Yet again the concept of free market is not for our experience and many multinational corporations do not even sell African products using prices established by the laws of supply and demand in a free market. Increased costs of production are not passed onto the consumers who buy the produce, instead they are sold from the source in Africa at a lower rate which means less income for African workers and businesses. The global market also sets a price on most of Africa's exports and so the higher production cost cannot be recouped. At the same time, a rise in productivity will not necessarily lower world prices by an increase in supply, because the demand may remain fairly small. Africa has mostly been caught in this economic cycle. This is a fundamental inequality in international trade and once this has been set up it is difficult to change. So the African economists are yet again called to reason together and define the contexts on which the International trade partnerships must be carried out. It could be our time to set up our trading systems and control our produce in more friendly for our own benefit and to build up sufficient national wealth to invest in our infrastructure. And industry so that our continent can be at par with the rest.

A fundamental oversight that we have witnessed also involves our constant loss of human resource to other continents. The African youth must stay in Africa in order to participate in the development process and in some countries, in the struggle to bring about good leadership that is unique and specific and must not keep wondering like the prodigal son across Europe and America. We must allow ourselves to be gainfully employed and engaged in productive activities that will make us realize a better economy. The Ghanaian youth must stand up and resist the urge to cross into Europe to partake of the pomposity and prestige that was brought about by the struggles and sweat of the young generation in Europe, and to begin similar processes that will ensure sufficient empowerment. The East African young men and women must roll their sleeves and demand to be involved right in their countries. Back in the days, history will remind us that when that time to salvage the oppressed and undignified man and woman under King Louis XVI's tight grip and aristocratic regime, the French young stars, middle men and lower class rose up and their voices were heard in 1789 when they staged the historic French Revolution whose consequences remain preface upon which revolutionary heralds would be told. Yet I am aware that earlier in 1783, the United States of America had staged what has been known as the American Independence Revolution. But the zest with which early days revolutions emerged and were sustained remains a tool that I would wish was transferred to our generation of the youth today! The Nigerian people must not allow themselves to be on record as the highest population of immigrants in Europe and America and of late in Asia. The young African in Central African Republic and the Congo must begin to realize that they are the voice of change and agents of unity that will cause a sporadic explosion of peace and harmony in that part of the world and choose to stay back in their land instead of running away to seek respite that last only like the dew. We must not take it for granted that we are the only continent that enjoys a youthful population majority in the world, but choose to deliberately aggregate ourselves into packs of influence that will transform leadership protocols into service. According to projection figures published in the UN data, Africa's population is expected to rise to 4.4 billion on lower scenarios by 2100 claiming one-third of the world's population. Presently, African has less than 1.5 billion people but will be around 2.5 billion by 2050. Another 50 years later, we shall double our projection! This calls for wisdom. We cannot wait until when we have no proper provision of social amenities to begin strategizing on management and governance. It has to begin now. And the people to begin it are the young generations. The fact of the matter is as much of Africa is still developing, and it contains some of the poorest countries on earth, the question on how it will sustain such massive population growth must be addressed as a matter of urgency.

Notably, the role of the African youth is drastically changing. Today, the youths face a myriad of challenges and opportunities in equal measure. The young people in our continent must be given the space and luxury of decision making to redefine the future that they want. This opportunity however must come through the informed guidance by our present role players in the various sectors of the economy. The strength of any society is within the strength and resolve of its youth. This society must therefore interrogate itself and pose the question- what investment are young people making in our continent today? Giving an informed opportunity to our young people will ensure a continuous delivery of stable leadership with a cognizant priority about the future because our young people must possess the power of foresight and the vision to visualize our society with an exactitude of a prophet. Unfortunately, the African youth seem to be interested in other continents than in Africa. Our young people have certainly lost the script of who they are and by extension, they role in the society. Our young people no longer celebrate our own things, including the African games. Today, the African continent has forgotten her football teams and has tuned into Westernized football clubs. Not that there is anything wrong with celebrating the clubs from the West, but this is a testament of a tragedy that Africa does not celebrate her own. A society that cannot have control over her future is no better than dead. We must not allow our continent to enter into this record because we have the capacity to prevent it from happening. We must wake this continent up of her slumber.

The Interesting Factor of Education and the Miseducation of the African People, is it by Design or Default? Choice or Alternative?

I will take on the African education further. Going forward, we must agree that taking thieves to colleges and training centres are only capable of making the best thieves in them. But at the same time, we have to realize that Africa depends on other continents to fund the education of her people. Africa cannot afford meaningful scholarships to the African populations and a big number of young Africans seeking to climb education ladder are faced with lack of financial cutesy to further their academic dreams. This does not stop African leaders from the thievery action seen in different sectors of government. Money is stolen day in day out, but we cannot educate our own people because we lack the money. We must redefine where we begin the whole process. The contexts on which the idealism of the African civilization has been choreographed is an ever complex subject that requires deep inspection with a view to underpinning the mismatch of the Africa education system and its failure to secure equal impact as did the other education systems, even though our system are heavily lifted from some of the systems seen to be working efficiently in the agenda of societal transformation. We must be alive to the fact that the knowledge from the West may not necessarily be a solution to our problems. When it is found to be incompatible with our needs and problems, we can groom our unique system of education that will address our specific challenges in conclusive and contextual manner rather than extrapolative deductive mechanisms. Such an indigenous system must be employed in the coaching, education and training of the African future leaders to offer the leadership that the content needs for prosperity and in turn tackle the unique problems of Africa. This education must allow the African young person to serve Africa. Evidence is available and painfully indicates that the grass is not always greener on the other side of the continent and the influx of the African manpower into abroad countries, contrary is creating confusion and jeopardy as leaders of other nations are also facing domestic challenges and therefore not prioritizing on the burgeoning number of the African immigrants. If our educational institutions can include entrepreneurship as a mandatory subject at all levels of education, more young people will be better equipped to create jobs and address the issue of high unemployment rather than relying on the government even when it is apparent that the government cannot be the sole employer of all her citizens. China has done it and we can see the taste of being unique in her progressive emergence as a developed country. India is doing it, Malaysia and Singapore did it and so are many other nations we have been trying to mimic. The jury is open and clear. It can be done. What we need to do is to add a little more spices to our science and technical based courses and upgrade institutions offering such courses. Africa has many brilliant people and I am sure that when their wealth of knowledge is utilized accordingly, there will be positive change.

Writing way back in the 1770s, Pope Alexander pointed out that:

> "A little learning is a dangerous thing. Drink deep, or taste
> not the Pierian Spring; their shallow draughts intoxicate
> the brain, and drinking largely sobers us again."

There is a sense in which I find meaning and relevance to this thought and I beg to utilize it as a preface to establish my understanding of the present education of the African nation in the foreign land. When Africa was invaded by the colonial warlords, there was a claim that they had come to do several things among them spread education, religion and trade. Whether one chooses to agree on this or not, it is well corroborated that they did not deliver on their promise in a manner that could help the indigenous Africans to be self-sufficient. Educating the African child on literature and subaltern mindset was only meant to equip them with knowledge only good enough to be subordinates and servants of the colonial masters. The knowledge on science and technology has remained a preserve for the few in the African context, borrowing from the colonial masters even when it is the Africans running their own education systems! Even with the realization that we can only gain much through science and technology, African remains infant in her pursuits to offer quality education based on neatly selected scientific background to her people. It is a pity to see the few number of Africans enrolled for courses in sciences and mathematics. And even if they are enrolled, the quality of the education they obtain remains debatable. There are consequences of this education that should be felt in the African soil several years after the continent has been engaged in the business of receiving and extracting an education of the west. Yet there is little to show for this cause as Africa remains behind the frontier of academia. I am aware that there are dedicated Africans who have exemplified themselves in this direction and are counted among the many with academic significance, but why is this enigmatic academic credentials and zest not featuring in the administrative functions of Africa? Why is it that whenever Africa tries to ride on her best economic crest she experiences a failure of catastrophic proportion? Why is it that the learned Africans cannot transform Africa into a better continent? What then is the power and influence of the western springs if it cannot sober up the minds and attitudes of a recipient? Of what role is it if even with the education we are still tightly engraved to our ethnic extractions and even our jobs are distributed along these basis, even when it is the elites with the power of distribution?

Why is it that Europe, America and the modern day Asia strategically employed the power of education and scientific innovations to create what we now see as the modern Europe, the modern day Dubai, Singapore, Norway, Korea, Kuwait, Indonesia among the leading nations but when it is about Africa, we shift the story and beg to use a different classification? We have to interrogate whether what we have as a form of education impacts any value and meaning to us, and our future or it is just disjointed tool that can only draw drops of features of an education program without impacting the fabric component of an individual. We need to know what we teach our young generations and, where necessary, adjust according to the pace of the world. We cannot apply the European wheel to our problems. What then is the value of an education if it cannot influence the fabrics of the consciousness of a society to begin implementing its contents in the direction of active development and offering a sense of hope and security? The need to reinvent a wheel with specifications for Africa is required. We cannot apply generic antidotes from other civilizations to our present diagnosis and hope to find cure, we have to obtain our antidotes right in Africa and blend it with the African culture and spirit so as to function on the African problem. Copy pasting on this will never work. America and her opinions will not shape the direction on which the African ship of development has to go. The EU or America can no longer dictate anymore the manner in which Africa needs to govern herself or give directions and orders as though it has been appointed into the supreme position of a prefect of the African continent. I say so and talk hard about these international agencies and governments because their commitment on the democratization of Africa and other developing nations has been compromised and characterized by behind-the-curtain schemes and treacheries, only for their own end gain. They have arrogated themselves the absolute power to direct the cause of action and our leaders have no thought but absolutely believe everything from them. But even so, the contributions of the global players have been present in Africa, but our issues remain glued to us regardless of the numerous years they will stay with us. You think I am against foreign partnerships on development? No. Rethink about it. It has to be the Africans themselves who must come out and utilize the power of their voices in creating the change just as Europe and America did. Nothing remains permanent and I believe our situation won't be the first. If Europe and America and the Asian world went through internal revolutions to be where they are today, nothing should persuade Africa that they will reap the fruits of justice, good governance, democracy, working systems and equality without an internal revolution. The characters who have negated our weights must undergo an expulsion from our systems, and I dare say that an internal revolution is an inevitable process for Africa to be an equal player in the global affairs.

Is it not Kofi Anan who once said that knowledge is power? Information is liberation. Education is the premise of progress, in every society, in every family? And is not Theodore Roosevelt who postulated that to educate a man in mind and not in morals is to educate a menace to society? Looking at these, I get the sense in which these insights were predicated. Not much has changed on the African curriculum several decades after self-governance. Africa continues to copy and paste western education curriculum and brags of a progressive education. An education must add value to the learner and to enable the learner appreciate their environment, it has to be customized to the realities of the environment and the context of the learner. We must have an education which we can identify with. Take for instance, in Africa, the books we use to teach our children are filled by names of missionaries and explorers from the West with every discoveries and findings in Africa. We are told of the first white man to discover a mountain, rivers or a lake or something in Africa, right under the noses of our forefathers! How possible? Does it mean our forefathers were unable to see the huge mountains protruding high in the sky? What did they do with their time? But we never mind. This education is not for our environment. The contents of our books are filled with these imaginary discoveries that should be only taught to in Europe. I am yet to find where the history of African great men and women and the African freedom fighters, who gave the European a great deal of their time, being taught to the European child. I have neither found, nor have I heard of a curriculum that exposes much about Africa in Europe, and if one would think otherwise, for a very long time, in the mind of many western nationals Africa is thought to be one country, despite the mention of the many African countries and leaders. Back in Africa, we praise the discoveries of the western missionaries. We are comfortable to teach our children that it is these white men who were the first men to see rivers passing right next to the places of residence of our forefathers. Africans have no pride in themselves. I submit that Africa must begin to understand herself. We cannot develop people.

Knowledge must be permanently resident in the minds of the Africa person and the mode of its transfer must mutate from the basic predominant old fashioned form and begin to diffuse systematically in a more robust and interactive way that will go along with influencing critical future insights and abilities. We must as a people grow from the beliefs that presuppose that knowledge is only functional when it is acquired in the Europe and USA, and begin to promote our continent and its values in order to attract other foreign nationals to learn from Africa. It does not meet purpose of argument when we have courses, even course such as African studies and African Linguistics and Sociology, taught to African by non-Africans in foreign land! I find this a little disturbing. However, I support the thought that we must allow ourselves the luxury of collaboration with other key players from outside Africa to diversify our development priorities with a rapidly shifting world. But even in our midst, we must be open, solvent and easily integrated in order to create an environment where intelligence is made s collective as possible for the ultimate benefit of all. This way, we shall be able to, in a more firm way, gain foresight of our society and walk in the isle of its sustainability. We must spar into action that wisdom that resides in the minds of our very own and utilize the power of togetherness to create a better society. No discipline is to be left out. The scientists must be brought on board, the geologists and anthropologists too must sit on this table as well as financial connoisseurs, all with a more critical discussion among themselves. Africa will be home to 38 of the 40 youngest countries in the world, with median populations under 25 years of age by 2050. Clearly, with this huge influx, considerable amount of investment must go into human development to unlock a demographic dividend present in this continent. We must ask the question; what innovative policies and programmes do young people want to see executed so that this growth will not result into a demographic time bomb for Africa? Yet even as the world believes that this is the century for the African Continent, Africans themselves have no grasp of what it takes to escape from destitution. The youth must be innovative without borders and they must be given the tools and power to exercise their expected role in the society in a more intense manner that triggers development.

I remain as strong in my belief as one needs to be in my persuasion that given time and good latitude of optimism, Africa can become great and I have no doubt in my hope that sooner or later we shall write different scripts about this land. For time without number Africa has demonstrated with a consistency of irreproachable magnificence that among her greatest challenges she has faced has to do with a unique absence of good-willed leadership, and this is not begged on the absence of good leaders from this continent but rather on the sudden proliferation of wrong individual who masquerading as leadership, and the unspeakable affinity of the African man and woman on the monstrous leader. We can talk about this over and over but an ultimate conclusion we shall arrive at is that the African person has tolerated this bad leader with a brave but misinformed hope that the misleader will by factors unknown to man be transformed and metamorphosize into a leader of hope and begin to do great exploits. The other bottleneck is the lack of a thinking Africa. I tend to alien myself to the school of thought that thinks that both the African person and the African leader, in a greater measure, are dissolved into a vacuum of absence of thought and this has displayed us dangerous. I once heard it being said that a big proportion of Africans and the African leaders don't think. I believe this is through, not in conjectural means but extensively, this can be debunked. The continent of Africa has constantly yearned to prove that deep inside her lies seeds of greatness waiting to germinate. It has now been provoked to unbridle the silent wealth of power that has been screaming for exposure several decades after her formation and self-rule. The recent formation of the African Continental Free Trade Area by 44 African heads of governments is a clear testament that there is finally some hope in the future prospects of Africa. But this is just an infant step. A lot more must be undertaken and pursued with the touch of excellence and dignity towards the realization of this pact. And this is where the challenge is on the African people.

How can Africa move from the present immobile and deactivated mode to a sporadic, spontaneous, vibrant, active and positively infectious position in the global description, where her energetic population does not have to migrate and become immigrants in other continents with the hope of gaining employment or better lives? I want to share a few things I believe must and should happen for the destiny of Africa to change dramatically.

1. Africa must begin to respect the laws of fair and transparent elections. Not until the African people will fully appreciate the need to have sanity in her electoral exercise, the periodic elections across the continent will remain meaningless and not able to inspire and socio-economic and political dynamism.

2. Africa must take up the responsibility of educating her people using efficient and effective education systems, fully equipped with modern applications and innovative features. By allowing other civilizations to define which education system works for her, the African continent presents herself as a jangle of dryness and elusive hope. There is need to prioritize our education for the good of our generations.

3. Africans must begin to define who she elects as her leaders in all spheres of life. I have stated here that the African voter is a character full of incredible humor. It is in this part of the world where wolfs are elected to take care of sheep.

4. The African population must be gainfully utilized to enhance growth and production in Africa. As it conversed over this book, Africa will only grow when her resources are utilized optimally. This must include the human resource, well equipped and developed for a mission-make Africa great!

5. Africans must take up on the responsibility of running the affairs of their land and begin to dictate what terms the continent has to be governed. On several occasions, we have allowed ourselves to be controlled and ruled on the remote control by other nations. This happens despite electing our own leaders. Why is it so difficult for Africans to elect responsible, charismatic and independent leaders? Well, I have a few cases that this kind of election has started to grip the continent, and wherever it has occurred, a ripple effect is visible. It remains my hope that this little ripple effect will grow in exponential terms to fill the whole continent.

6. The African people must strive to do more, sweat more and labour hard in the fields of her economic battle and must never give up the will. Nothing shall ever come on a silver platter. We have to work hard and earn our growth by it. The potential that lies in this continent cannot be fully achieved if we became slothful and idle in our work. We have the duty to work extra hard to make our hyped development come true.

It is upon us to set the rules that will govern our democracies and migrate from the present foreign prototype systems of governance that are irreproducible, irretraceable and unsystematic. Foreign diplomats must not be confused to be our reference standards and allowed to meddle with our priorities because history has remained constant on their agendas and several accounts encapsulate the deceit and frame that they hide under the table. They may shout about one thing and the other, but that never solves our issues. They may give directions and opinions from time to time but still have their intentions fixed and secure. We must be weary that we have in our midst a group of people who celebrate when things go wrong in our house! We must behave as the uniformed Israelites who wondered who had sent Moses without their knowledge to prefect them in a foreign land. We must do things than on the basis of evidence will disapprove the rest of the world and earn our bridal position in the table of modern civilizations.

I am reminded of a song by Nas and Damian Marley Africa must wake up. I choose to deliberately share the following lines of the song as borrowed from a reliable source:

> Africa must wake up The sleeping sons of Jacob For what tomorrow may bring May a better day come Yesterday we were Kings Can you tell me young ones Who are we today, yeah now

These words have been selected on purpose and I believe that the agitation present in this song is to invoke the spirits of the African minds to begin to take up their positions in the arena that shape up life and existence. They remind one of the prestigious position Africa held during her time. Things are unfortunately different today but not hopeless. When you take a close look at Africa and try to understand the continent from the perspective of other civilizations or continents if you may, whether you are from America or Asia, the contextualization is one and the same. Among the advanced sets of problems facing Africa, you will notice that endless poverty is given prominence. But is Africa poor? No. I have disclosed that Africa is the most graced continent with a myriad of resources and potentials, including the human capital and natural gifts such as oil and lucrative mineral ores. But why do the international humanitarian organizations and formations, including UNICEF, WHO, Flying Doctors, Doctors without Borders, among others, continue to thrive on portraying this continent as a dark poor continent? Well, not hard on anything. But why do the international organizations' vigor and zest more felt in Africa? It is so because we need their help. Yes. After over 55 years of self-rule we are still far from developing from our infancy to adulthood. We still find ourselves under the merciless treatment of foreign nationals who have investments in our land as we labour and toil to serve in their investments. We are still treated as lesser beings among other races. Africans are still subjected to all manner of despicable inhuman treatments. Why are the Africans not objecting to certain unfounded theories advanced by these organizations? It is because Africans believe that they are poor and have been drawn deep inside the darkest box of poverty and the only thing in mind is to remain in the state of poverty and despair, even if some analyses indicate growth and advancement on literally nothing significant? A mindset of economic servitude and unending poverty. Not even African leaders have a dream. While the international organizations have a vision for the continent, the African leaders have abused the role of these bodies and have blatantly neglected their roles in service provision to the people to these bodies while they have the task of accumulating resources for their own sake. This is why I am persuaded that these organizations must begin to allow the African leadership to transform and take up their responsibilities. The baby must be allowed to walk on its own and permitted to fall then when it can't rise up, one has to hold its arms in support. We must not allow to be offered the fish all the time, let us seek to learn how to catch the fish ourselves and feed on our own. Meanwhile, their complementation will be welcomed. But as long as the international community and development partners continue to assume the bulk of humanitarian response activities, conflict management, disaster and every emergency response, the Africa leaders will continue to take their share out of the public coffers and forget there are fundamental issues of priority to their people which require their undivided attention.

The Giant in the Slumber Land must be Provoked to Stay Awake Otherwise it Perishes...

The African natural resources and evident wealth cannot permit me to stoop low to conclude that Africa is a poor continent and therefore the presence of the international support group is justified. On the contrary, Africa should be doing and offering a lot of help to the entire world. We have chosen to describe ourselves this way and it is only us to delete these words by demonstrating that indeed our wealth is inherently ours and was designed for our greatness. Second to our wound is our over-dependence on international aid. I talked previously about the Kenyan debt scenario and how this debt has made every living Kenyan appear as an international beggar on the streets. In order to get Africa to her feet, International Aid was formed. But in the end, "international economic partners" and aid lenders begun to control the African leaders through such aids. In unprecedented occurrence, the African leaders relinquished their political leadership responsibilities on their subjects and even nations. Many of them for a long time have sat back and soothed off their duties to guide development and instead, pegged the running and growth of the economies of the countries on the basis of international aid, instead of utilizing such aids to spark their own development that would bring about self-sustainability and economic independence. What I see is a micromanagement of the African economies by foreigners, and if there is any doubt on this, the recent emergence of the Chinese philanthropic economic ambitions will deliver my point. Africa has been micromanaged by the United

States, and Europe and presently, whether a majority are beginning to indicate a change of allegiances to the Asian superpowers, the concept of micromanagement remains viable and true. This is regrettably a deleterious form of imperialism as it imprisons the minds and aspirations of the African leaders, forcing them to reason from the narrow scope of aid. It is an imperialism of stupendous magnitude to have your leaders imprisoned by other civilizations and they start to behave as secondary class individuals before them. These homage have seen a lot of infiltration of "dangerous" customs and social order penetrate into the African soil. Only a few African leaders managed to dispel these strong influence and out rightly rebuked the elites for forcing irrelevant customs on the African people. A majority however have over the years been subservient and fallen to these customs which are irrelevant and tertiary in demand to the vast majority of the Africans. I always say that African still needs to provide basic things to her people and should not be cajoled to offer luxurious stupidity to her masses on the simple basis that Europe and America are doing so.

I am in positive agreement with the Ghanaian president Nana Akufo-Addo when he says Africa cannot continue to thrive and develop on the basis of foreign aid. People have to develop themselves. It is ridiculous and regrettably shameful that several years after self-rule we have continued to punch below our economic weight and we have kept looking for aid and help from other nations which, in the order of priority, did the right things to spar their economy. This continued seeking of help does not only stop with economic aid. No. The African leaders have continued to seek help on how to fight against corruption committed right here in Africa by African themselves! There is now no difference and nothing on which Africa does not seek support. Most military in Africa is heavily supported by other continents, America on the top. But even when this support is won, there is a snail move at ensuring accountability of the support funds. Africa is synonymous and has a huge reputation on corruption, and the quest to bend low to fight the corruption perpetrated by simple individuals whose desire is to ensure that whatever effort Africa makes is negated as soon as it is thought of. I am convinced that Africa's further transformation, Africa's advancement, progress and success rest simply in the acknowledgement, validation and mainstreaming of Africa's own traditional, authentic, original, indigenous knowledge. It is hinged in education, in research, in policy making and across sectors. We have to customize for ourselves our own systems of doing things. We cannot keep applying copy and paste solution method. We cannot develop successful agricultural styles for Africa when we paste the agricultural methods applied in Europe and America simply because we have to understand that Europe and America are different from Africa. This is not going to be easy for a people who are used to being told how to think, what to do, how to do what they have to do. It will be a task delivering this to a people long subjected to intellectual guidance and the direction of others. This is the task we must strive to do in order to make us progress. It can never be greater than the will, the power and the zeal and enthusiasm we have inside of us. It is never enough to think outside the box. We must think without the box. It is Mahatma Gandhi who proclaimed that if you can think you need no teacher. We can think this, clearly well I am persuaded.

This drives me to my third point. Lack of true servanthood leadership. The African leader can be well described as a figure who does not have a grasp on the major problems of the people and do not understand the basic principles or rules that govern the destiny of a people. This issue has been the chorus of this article and I have advanced what I consider solutions to the situation. But in conclusion, it will be needful to remind us that bad leadership will always result into suffering. A leadership that lacks wisdom cannot champion for development and it is high time the African men and women begun raising from amongst ourselves men and women of wisdom, upright thoughts and integrity to lead us. Yet it remains unexplained how the continent has remained a centerpiece for war. Even at family levels, the continent has registered concerns at the levels of intolerance against themselves. It is here where a brother kills a brother, a husband murders his entire family, a son his father and so on, right at the family level. I have always wondered why these have to happen at this generation and time. Why should a people who have lived alongside each other for generations of time suddenly decide to attack their neighbours? Yet some of these conflicts date back to many years ago. Are these conflicts fueled by ethnic intolerance? Who creates the ethnic classification and decides which ethnic groupings have to be eliminated? Who is this who has the monopoly of wisdom to judge men on the basis of their ethnic extraction and wedge war against them? And who are we to constantly be fueled to fight amongst ourselves without realizing that we all have equal opportunity to live? As I write this, the South Sudan is at war against herself, Nigerian ethnic clashes are unending with the constant manslaughter of people by an illegal sect and there is a constant political threat in Algeria, Morocco, Ethiopia and the list is endless. Many African countries have the illegal sects and their mission is to cause chaos and disruption among people. Who are they? Where do they come from? Who funds them? What is the source of their sophisticated weaponry? Why is Africa comfortable at fighting against itself? And why should they continue as terror groups among us if they are from us? The elites rash and inform us that these conflicts are fueled by ethnic intolerance? Ethnic intolerance? Sons orchestrating mass murder of lives in their own very villages is an ethnic intolerance? I am not persuaded it should be termed so. Why is the African voice silent against visible perpetrators of conflicts in the DR Congo? Why has the part of Africa remained in constant turmoil since the assassination of Patrice Emery Lumumba? Why is the Somalia war stricken nation despite her rich natural resources? Who benefits from these resources? What is the role of the peace keeping forces employed at the courtesy of the UN and other African nations? Why has the Darfur remained a hotspot yet it is the same people who live here? Shall these questions be answered? Yet at the global periscope, Africa remains to be a theatre of war. And we are not limited to these kinds of war only. Africa is at war with poverty that never ends. She is at a losing war with endemic diseases including malaria and AIDS is getting out of control.

What has always surprised me is that no African country currently manufactures ammunitions and the sophisticated weaponry we have seen engaged during these ill-fated tribal or ethnic conflicts. They are sourced from the back door and in most cases under the assistance of some kind. But appropriately, nobody has been found culpable for the massive crime against humanity which continues to escalate time in and again. While remaining true to my reviews and the long term observations across the continent, it has been clearly showed that political arrangements that facilitate better representation of ethnic groups in governments have been of significant help in resolving conflict in some countries and should be more widely used in dealing with conflicts in the continent.

Africans must remain vigilant and adequately updated on the issues shaping up the world stories especially with relevance to governance and economic growth but also of importance to help define their global understanding of the external environment. Africans can no longer be at the isolation plateau of awareness. With the benefit of the social network, the continent must begin to create useful links with other continents to learn the positive lessons from them. The media must play its central role in educating the population based on material facts with an aim to spur the critical development in the society. In the recent years and even presently, it is almost hard to tell what exactly the role of the African media is because in my opinion, Africans have no control over their media, and the media seems to be a tool utilized immensely by some groups for unfounded motives which are of negative consequences to the people. We must have a media that is vibrant and fervent in her quest to create a just society. We must allow the media industry to grow far above mere journalism that breeds discord and propagates indecency among us. We must allow the freedom of the media to be exercised with the hope that the media will remain an eye of the society and point the attention of the general society to the evils propagated by unwanted characters in our midst. The media must remain both neutral and unbiased in her functions but this must ensure that substance of relevance is diffused into the society. I have had problems with the conduct of some media outlets with regard to their content. Some media firms attempt to engage the public on completely irresponsible, immature and irrelevant debates and discussions of least consequences and less priority. They have missed the opportunity to educate their adherent audience on quality material information and impactful content, rendering them toxic and regrettable. That is often the media we have. A complete failure in a society which is described as developing. For how long shall the African media continue to wonder in the infancy of journalism and be an ever present adolescent in the coverage of societal issues? My response to some has been that Africa and her readers cannot continue to be paraded as consumers of every content; both ill and good. We must select what material we wish to consume and the closer it is to our circumstances and quest, the more relevant it becomes. But the social media has always ran over the counter in its ability and continues to do more harm than good in our society. The huge rush to magnify certain inhuman acts and portray them as progressive changes in societal development is a retrogressive lapse in our tight moral values. Everything must be allowed to begin from some point. We cannot suddenly turn into entertainment theaters while social injustices are conducted against the people we need to defend. When the local media fails to live to their expectation, we obviously expect the worst to come from the so called international media. And for a fact, the international media has never found something positive about African and her people and has constantly struggled to portray the continent as a backward space. These international media firms choose to ignore facts and baselines and instead give several doubtful and adulterated accounts about the situation in African. In the end, the beautiful continent of Africa is portrayed as a backward land whose impact is insignificant in the global face. We are aware of the problems we face as a people but curing a wound cannot be achieved by increasing the size of the wound or by increasing the pinch of salt to apply. We must begin to develop interest about Africa as the rest of the world have demonstrated their interest about our continent. An exactitude proportion is required and not only that, reporting accounts by themselves are only meant for information, and cannot include solutions, especially when these accounts are compromised and misguided as we have mostly seen. Today, Africa does not tell her story. Instead, the African story is told by the BBC, the CNN, the Voice of America, the Aljazeera and other international newsrooms yet there is no shortage of media firms and journalistic frames all over Africa. These foreign media firms tell the African story from their own perspective and interest. Nothing significant about Africa is focused in most of their news. All we see is negative history that brings no hope but continues to ridicule and demean Africa and her leadership. The African media must now begin to tell the story of Africa passionately to awaken the conscious and awareness of the African society. It is through positive, robust, dedicated and concrete media that the situation of Africa will find a realist focus and attention.

It is my presumption that I now have more why's than it is necessary from my readers. Am not sure if I could also unpack these fundamental concerns adequately and with the utmost depth of description requisite of them. Nevertheless, one thing for a fact is, we are not limited by our circumstances. Not at all. In fact, before the emergence of colonial warlords and the so called superpowers, the African societies coexisted in peace and deep founded harmony. I am aware there were pockets of clashes here and there but often the elders chose peace over fighting unless the latter was unavoidable. Several communities lived in harmony and there was sufficient provision back then. This is not to say we were better off then than we are today. The world has advanced almost in all its forms and foundations and I am of the view that Africa was not going to remain in the state it was in in the 18th Century even if the colonial societies did not come for the very reasons they did. One can therefore not claim that Africa did not have this or that, but it does not matter now. We have passed some critical tests. Political, economic and societal structures existed in the African society and were performing in accordance with the views of the people. Back then not many discoveries had been made about the wealth of resources lying in the belly of Africa except for the superficial trades that took place. It is often forgotten that the first civilization to visit and take Africans out of the comfort of their homes were the Arabs. When you look at the contact of Africa and the Arabs, one will single out the Trans-Saharan trade and the enslavement of the Africans by the Arabs as its most poisonous impact. Africans were taken out of Africa and were made to work as slaves in other continents. It is painful to note but we began from somewhere. It was not the intent of the Arabs to colonize Africa. Trade was perpetuated on commodities and Africa sold and exchanged what they had for the Arab goods. Among what Africa had was a juvenile population which could be offered as commodities for cheap labor in other nations. Africans sold themselves to other civilizations. Sad but it happened. I am not aware of any other continent which sold her people to other continents. Later in the course of time the Portuguese came to Africa and challenged the Arabs influence. But they also perpetuated slavery. Slave trade was turned into slave raids and millions of Africans were "stolen" from their land into new land where they toiled. Portugal intervened in local wars among African kingdoms hoping to get abundant mineral riches, imposing a protectorate. They tried this with the Monomotapa kingdom in the present Zimbabwe, were present in the present Congo where they used the Kongo kingdom early with a similar scheme against the Ndongo kingdom. They were convinced that the black soil was in dare need of governance and rulers and that they were the best appointed humans to rule the Africans. They counted as inconsequent the political structures eminent among many African societies and devised modes and means to change the systems into their own.

The Dutch came and founded their space, the English came and started trading in West Africa, but came into conflict with Portuguese troops. The French were also present from the 1620s and expelled the Dutch from Senegal. In 1650, Swedish merchants founded Swedish Gold Coast in modern Ghana following the foundation of the Swedish Africa Company (1649). The Dano-Norwegian colonized the Danish Gold Coast, from 1674 to 1755. The Spaniards came and by 1777 they had signed a treaty with the Portugal in which they were granted portions of the Guinea. The explorative works by the European nations ended up in a struggle and later partition of Africa as the African countries were parceled out and shared among the powers. It is not my intention to awaken the dark memories of the colonial times but there is a sense in which we have to constantly remind ourselves our history because history is rich and a steadfast teacher in a society. I keep reminding myself of the backgrounds upon which our liberation was hinged and find myself irritated when I hear of theft of public funds, inefficient public service delivery, lack of accountability at the public sector, inability of the African countries to educate her citizens and high dependence on foreign aid, among other the vices going on. Yet there remains no accountability in the African nations.

The coming of the colonizers crushed the existing socio-economic and political systems that was increasingly advancing in Africa. The African land became a commodity for grab and it happened that African societies were divided and caused to fight among themselves. Well this is the task of memories. I want to end it there but a little history is good. The trans-Atlantic slave trade caused the forceful removal of millions of Africans from the continent. This number included a large percentage of skilled tradesmen, women and youths from a range of occupations and professions who were making their contribution to African societies. Without this workforce, African societies themselves remained conscripted weakened and powerless. Yet they participated in the building of other nations in forced, exploitative, extractive and pernicious labour.

Africa had trading systems which had developed over hundreds of years – well before Europeans ever arrived on their shores. Europeans destroyed these systems in large areas of Africa when they developed the trade in enslaved Africans. Local systems were badly affected and overwhelmed by the demands of the new trade in enslaved Africans, a trade imposed by the better developed guns and ships of the Europeans. But one can easily tell why Africa has for all these decades remained underdeveloped and poor to an extent that President Donald Trump of the USA cannot help but describe African nations with derogative words like he did, which in my view are not meant to insult Africans but should be utilized to engage the Africans on the finer points of governance, nationalism and socio-economic and political freedom. The Europe's past (and present) exploitation of Africa played a significant role in exposing the African wealth and resources to the lashing appetite of the developed world. Before the Europeans arrived in Africa, Africa had vibrant economic, social and political structures. These were severely disrupted by Europeans to create wealth for themselves. We saw it happen with the Belgium where the present war epicenter of Congo has remained in the conflict mode and a fighting country can best explain her. It was in the desire of the liberators of Congo that it be democratic and a republic, and these titles were assumed, later what we see is different, but we cannot appeal to have the preceding titles be forgotten. We still describe it as democratic even if nothing democratic is known to happen in it, and it enjoys the title of a republic against her spirits. Yet Africans have chosen to be silent about it.

European dominance over most of Africa through the Trans-Atlantic slave trade lasted 440 years, from 1444 to 1885. When it was abolished, colonialism took over and there is a way in which the

African nations have never been the same after this event that lasted until 1994 in the case of South Africa. The consequences are, Africans got encouraged to wage war against one another and conduct raids, instead of building more peaceful links. To date, there is no peace is several part of the African continent even with several generations after slave trade, yet the perpetrators never come out to apologize and end the animosity. By the time that Africa had escaped the shackles of the slave trade and entered the colonial era, its main export was raw cotton. Yet its main import was manufactured cotton cloth! This remarkable irony points not only to technological advance in Europe but also, and most importantly, to the stagnation of technology in Africa owing to the trade with Europe. It is clear that the Europeans did not want African states to develop their own technology or otherwise, the African leaders are not still prepared to develop their own technology. They did not want them to be able to make their own manufactured goods. It is still the same with the cocoa, tea coffee and many other indigenous African produce industries and I hope that with the intensification of food value chain programs, and attempts by Ghanaian business lots and other zealous African traders to begin processing their own produce will end some of these absurd scenarios and self-imposed servitude. The only way for the African nations and their leadership's desire to develop Africa will be reviewed on their legitimate response to creating technology hubs in the continent without constantly seeking out for unsolicited technological aid and machinery from other civilizations. Likewise, the genuine support from the rest of the world including Europe and presently China, which is on an unexplained expedition to control Africa, will be monitored on their readiness to allow Africa to develop her own systems without rushing up with ad hock solutions to the issues confronting Africa.

You will easily notice that my concerns are in the neighborhood of this fact. My argument and I am sure it is well corroborated, is that Africa has never freed herself from the domination by the conceptual West and of lately the Arabs and China. In the late 16th century and in the 21st century, the relationship between the west and Africa has been primarily one of exploitation. International trading agreements with Africa have been unfair on African countries. These agreements have been overly influenced by western big businesses and of lately the Chinese. Such unfair agreements and relationships have allowed individual African officials to get rich while the region sells itself cheaply and develops no infrastructure. This relationship of exploitation has been a common feature of the European intervention in Africa. It started with the arrival of the missionaries, and continued with the arrival of European merchants and mercenaries, and most lately, with the western multinational corporations. It is surprising that at this time and age, the Africans seem not to have learnt anything from such agreements and when the Chinese emergence into Africa is characterized by similar but even sophisticated schemes, we should deeply get worried.

Who will Feed Africa? Herself or Her Neighbours?

According to FAO, the Sub-Saharan Africa (SSA) region accounts for more than 950 million people, approximately 13% of the global population. This calls for fresh thoughts. But despite ongoing transformation of the region's economies, agriculture remains a crucial sector providing livelihoods for millions of people. Regional differences in the structure and development stage of agriculture reflect the vast agro-ecological, economic, political and cultural differences across the continent. Undernourishment has been a long-standing challenge, with uneven progress toward food security across the region. While food security enjoys a massive political prominence across Africa, the efforts undertaken to implement its realization are barely commensurate and target fix to bring about any realistic scales of success. Certainly, there must be committed interest by the African leadership to take control of their agriculture and the formal as well as the informal sectors of the economy. The continent cannot afford to ride on the back of the rest of the world decades after decades through aid and grants, yet it enjoys massive allocation of every natural wealth, including wildlife, minerals and pristine climate that favors productive agriculture and a hub of energetic human resource capability.

Development of the region's agricultural sector is being shaped by rapid population growth, urbanization and rural diversification, an associated structural transformation from farm to non-farm employment, the rise of a middle class, and increasing interest (both domestically and globally) in the continent's farmland. The good news would be that total agricultural production in this region is projected to expand by 2.6% p.a. In contrast with past production increases, which overall were driven by area expansion, an increasing share of future production growth will come from improved productivity. Inclusive development that improves the productivity of small-scale meanly resourced farmers will be needed, while creating broader rural development opportunities. These are the areas our research and technological advancement should critically lay focus on in order to improve our expectations. It is worth to take cognizance of the fact that while the outlook for agriculture in Sub-Saharan Africa is broadly positive, it could be much improved by more stable policies across the region, by strategic public and private investments, notably in infrastructure, and by suitably adapted research and extension. Such investments could improve access to markets, reduce post-harvest losses, and make needed inputs more widely available. The point is, we cannot go it alone. We need the international partnership, but we have to redefine our role in this arrangement. A partnership that is formed out of the good will to spar our economy is desirable. Not one whose prime intent is to debate on how the African wealth and resources will be redistributed among key global players while Africa remains in her sorry state of affairs. A partnership that will recognize that Africa is and can also be a dinner in the dinner table of economic advancement and civilization, and that her capacity to defend her people is not junior to that of other continents. Our policy making frameworks in these sectors must begin to rise above the occasion and deliver tangible products out of the constant global encounters. We would not wish to see our leaders invited in global arena just to be present for the sake of fulfilling an international outlook purposes, but as key players and contributors to the world's economy. The advent of the African Continental Free Trade Area must acquire the reception is ought to in the eyes of every African and we should hold it with two arms, guard its intent with intimate jealousy and ensure its progress at all cost. And this must be the unity time for Africa.

In a nutshell, the African agenda must find true bearers and messengers of goodwill with the agility and bravery of latter-day missionaries. We need leaders and not misleaders. We need teachers and not cheaters. The state of intra-African trade is shocking. Africa trades at no more than 20% within herself but expects to develop and grow to compete the rest of the world. We need servants and not masters who will understand that Africa must begin to trade with her own and make a decision to exploit her resources widely. Servants who will promote intra-African trade as well as trans-African trade with the carefulness our economic engagement requires and those who will never become subservient to the agitation of the conceptual West, the Chinese and rapidly now, the Arabs. We need servants who will be present at the dinner table of equality, presenting Africa as a continent of worth celebrating, and not being present for the sake of meetings or as objects and materials to be shared, in assemblies whose deliberation primarily is to parcel out Africa among the dinners. Or even carriers of dint of tokenisms provided under empathy and sympathy. Our leaders must take the seats at the dinner table as equal dinners and must never take the waiter's seat. We must end the mindset of tokenism that Africa has held herself on for a very long time. This calls for proactive, visionary and focused leadership. Not mere well-doers whose mission is cloudy and impregnated by vagueness that has no umbilical cord to the African dreams and aspirations. We don't need double standard individuals whose pronouncements today cannot be used as references of their positions tomorrow. We need people who speak with one voice and whose hearts and beliefs are never melted by mere threats and short term peripheral ablation of pomposity and pleasure. Such are the guys who must run our economies. These are the ones we must place in our best team for us to win in the first round of the game. We must say enough is never enough until we clear out the belch of the gluttony of these misleaders. Africa must wake up, take up herself and be the institution it deserves to be in the face of the earth. Countries undergoing adolescent tantrums must metamorphosize with speed to pave way for their maturity and liberation in order to achieve economic liberty. Genuine and beneficial democracy must be realized in all African countries for this to happen.

The African Women and Youth Platform; Challenges and Achievements... more Empowerment Struggles?

Another area that we must focus on is youth and women empowerment. Mahatma Gandhi, speaking about women empowerment stressed the role of women in the development of the society. Women are, in words of Gandhi, are the companion of men, gifted with equal mental capacity. He asserts that to call her a weaker sex is a libel; a man's injustice to a woman! Across Africa, this category of people have been sidelined from the past and their contribution to decision making, even in critical matters has been neglected despite being a critical formation of the entire population. The African male has remained a dominant but sessile species whose efforts needs to be complimented and supplemented in equal measure. The rise of women participation across African must be acknowledge but while doing so, it must be pointed that this has not been fully achieved and quite a number of African countries are yet to achieve gender equality. It is not lost on me that other civilizations are also struggling with this concept, and that Africa just begun walking through her isle of prospects and is not yet an equal ally or at par with the rest of the world. What I must discuss, and we need to be aware of, is that we cannot afford the luxury of procrastination. Again we cannot ever be at the infancy stage year in year out. We must give our young people and women the opportunity to take significant roles in our society. The reality is women's participation has registered positive improvement with notable pitfalls since 2005. Achievements noted include increased awareness, policy reforms, improved legislative frameworks, and institutional development at the national level in many countries. Positive undertakings include the establishment of national policies and strategies for gender equality; adherence to international and regional instruments for the protection of the human rights of women; increased diversity in the mechanisms promoting and monitoring attention to gender equality; attention to resource allocations through gender-sensitive budgeting; the recognition of the critical role played by NGOs in awareness-raising, advocacy, monitoring and programme delivery; and efforts to engage the male gender more actively in the promotion of gender equality. This is an area our global partners have constantly seconded our motion and it's a good indictment. Though there remains dint of challenges, the fight against gender equality will soon be won, and in this note, we have to reasonably think that gender equality means both sexes are according similar treatment. Overdosing either of the two with particular traits at the expense of the other might eventually jeopardize the space of the other.

One critical element that is regrettable is that over the ten years since the adoption of the Beijing Platform for Action by the Fourth World Conference on Women in 1995, a large gap still remains between policy and practice in the issues of enhancing women participation in development on the global scale. Discriminatory practices and negative public attitudes towards the advancement of women and gender equality have not changed at the same pace as policy, legal and institutional frameworks remains registered in many developing countries, although we are turning on to a new era on this. The Commission on the Status of Women, at its forty-ninth session in 2005, adopted a Declaration in which governments pledged to undertake further action to ensure the full and accelerated implementation of the Platform for Action and the outcome of the twenty-third special session. These enhance pronouncements and deliberations must not remain in the archives and monuments but must begin to cascade in every arc of the continent and the world at large, to draw in the undoubted truth, that, when offered the opportunity and support, women, can be smart and effective leaders of the society since they bare the greatest responsibility in the formation and sustenance of any society. A lot has to be achieved to ensure that we register impressive strides on women empowerment across the globe, and particularly in Africa where development issues takes focus with the role of women on the central dice.

Women must have access to positive power and leadership opportunities for our societies to grow. They must receive the kind of education and training their male counterpart receive, and their empowerment must not be seen an extension of favor but a normal encounter in human development, just as it has happened with the male category in every society. We must allow our women and young people to drive the economies of our cradle lands and not to be utilized for purposes of projecting devastating poverty and miseries in our societies. That time is now. We cannot condone the danger of gender exclusion. We must offer jobs in equal terms and conditions among males and females. The youths must be gainfully engaged in serious economic issues and this must rise above just engagement. We must offer our young people the deliberate will and trust to contribute meaningfully to the establishment of a stronger and victorious society. I have witnessed a number of projects started with the intentions to empower the youths and in most cases, frankly, I have felt disappointed and cheated. The question that I always struggle with is of what impact will the 'cup-bearing services' often offered to young people be to the economy and even to themselves? The youths cannot be gainfully engaged through cleaning streets and being employed as hand tools and other such mean related duties. It must not be engagement for the sake of it. Quality of the purpose duty is vital. They must be properly educated and trained to serve in the prime sectors of the economy. They must be given the best education in order to develop their skills and interest in driving the economy. When I see old guards who have stayed in power continue to be recycled into every form of service without shame and thoughtful regard to the many young people struggling to get access to jobs, many questions linger in my mind. Our old men and women must begin to pave way to allow a smooth transition of the young people as they, when qualitatively trained, bring forth a breath of new experience which is in tandem to the current wavelength the world is moving with. Old experiences can be utilized as a way to build on past mistakes, but cannot never be substitutions for the new era rapid growth that requires sophistication in technology and innovations.

I am still optimistic as I am honest, yet faithful to my boundaries of thoughts. It is serious and we have to do it. And a point to remember is that this must not only be in Africa. Our people must begin to receive the recognition we deserve and not to be employed for the sake of employment. We should begin to take up our roles in the global organizations and allow our voices to be heard unequivocally and steadfastly. We must now rise up to serve the world and not continue to be saved because every development must be progressive and one cannot afford to remain a toddler for the rest of their life because infancy is the lowest stage in life and one has to graduate adequately into maturity in order to develop a better understanding of his surroundings. This calls for a change of attitude. But the questions remain, is Africa and her people ready to exhibit the nature of personality that encompasses these responsibilities? Are our youths ready and willing to be in school and learning institutions and to be trained based on useful material and not be pets and dump ground for illicit social malnutrition from the other parts of the world? Are we as a people committed to certain values that will allow our global image to shine with a dazzling of the sun and to depict our true self in a more transparent and diligent manner? Are we willing to elect into office men and women who on the basis of their conduct will earn international respect and not constantly be publicly mortified on the account of their misconduct? Are we willing to begin using our own conviction to elect leaders of character and the content of their brains and not on the basis of the depths of their pockets or ethnic extractions? These are fundamental areas we must express our potion on and this must be known.

One will note that such empowerment agenda must not sideline educating the women in key terms and components of the society and allowing them unhindered access to critical areas of responsibilities. I commend the women who have risen to the occasion and showed exemplary leadership enigma and prowess in areas the society has reserved in the past for male dominance. Yet it must be remembered that the role of the African women was not predefined as of lesser position in the society. Evidence is available that in many African societies, the struggles for liberation were led by women who played indispensable role in the campaigns for national liberation and their continuing efforts in the present century is worth noting hence should be permitted on a larger latitude. It is only the colonizers who failed to recognize the women and their substantial role in our society. This unrecognition and their fundamental misunderstanding of the extent of women's role and their participation in society and the economy served as the impetus for women's participation in resistance movements. But we should not act like the imperialists did in the African dark days. A new dawn had been decreed in Africa and changes must be realized in all spheres. The sky is bright with hopeful wishes to all the African women. We must maximally capitalize this gesture.

History remains rich and unbiased and it reminds us that on the 9th day of August, 1956, some 20,000 women in South Africa marched from various regions to the apartheid capital of Pretoria. They represented a cross-section of women, most of whom were African, who resided and worked in both urban and rural areas of the country. Throughout the 20th century women in South Africa resisted the policies of the European settler-colonial rule under both British and Boer domination. As early as 1908, African women fought against racist laws that prohibited the brewing and distribution of traditional beverages, outlawed so that the men could be lured into beer halls and drained of their wage earnings. Women boycotted and picketed the beer halls, forcing many to close. They demanded that profits from the establishments be utilized to develop housing and amenities for the African people relegated to the townships by the racist colonial system. Indeed, it was the women-initiated struggle against the pass laws that sparked a broad-based mass movement during the 1950s. The major demand of the women's march on Pretoria was to abolish the passes that controlled the movement of Africans inside their own country. The women-led struggles were protracted and quite a number of them were imprisoned yet they kept the will alive.

It was not only in South Africa. Women's struggles also took place in various forms in many African states from the 1950s through the early 1990s, when the last vestiges of white-minority rule were eliminated in southern Africa. A major effort took place in 1960 when the All-African Women's Conference (AAWC) was formed in Accra, Ghana. Ghana in 1960 was considered the fountainhead of national independence and Pan-Africanism. During his time, Kwame Nkrumah, the leader of the

Convention People's Party, relied heavily on women in the urban and rural areas during the struggle for independence and the postcolonial period. It is true that the African women held a firm position in the production and agricultural sectors of the economy.

It reminds us of the events that took place in the country that became a political mecca for the African Women participation in the process of their nation. While addressing the very first African women congress, Nkrumah posed the question: "What part can the women of Africa and the women of African descent play in the struggle for African emancipation? And added "You must ask these questions not by word of mouth but by action — by positive action, which is the only language understood by the detractors of African freedom." Back then it was realized that as early as 1940s, the women in China were advanced in all spheres of useful activity and enjoyed equal rights with men politically, economically, culturally, socially and domestically. Women went on to play pioneering roles in other African liberation struggles in Angola, Mozambique, Zimbabwe, Kenya, Morocco, Namibia, Algeria, Tanzania, Guinea, Nigeria and Sierra Leone as well as many other states. They were part and parcel of the struggle. In Kenya, women were not left behind. They formed the Mau-Mu women wing where they staged impossible resistance to colonial imperialism. But where did the vigor and the zeal demonstrated by the women during the African emancipation go? Where did the spirit to fight it out and gain access in public offices get displaced? Today I see many countries in Africa struggling with gender equality and they have created positions reserved specifically for women in order for them to be in tandem with the constitutional requirements of gender equality. Is it that the African voter does not find pleasure in electing women into positions of power? Or is it that women are no longer as vigorous, bold and reliable as they were? The African Union declared 2010 the beginning of the "Decade of Women (2010-2020)" on the continent and even this seem not to be receiving the kind of reception it deserves.

But what is more? In the land of Angola, the Mbundu Kingdom had their female star, Ana de Sousa Nzinga Mbande who came to power as an ambassador after demonstrating an ability to tactfully defuse foreign crises, and she regained control of the Portuguese fortress of

Ambaca. But I need to point out that despite these classical evidences, the struggle for liberation for women has remained an ever green subject where in some countries such as Libya, they're forming private aid agencies, agitating for a role in the country's nascent political system and this seems to be a long fight. They need to be supported. Today she is remembered in Angola for her political and diplomatic acumen, as well as her brilliant military tactics. One can go on and on and talk of the present evidence. Then I can imagine of Liberia. The first African country to produce a female head of state and government; Ellen Johnson Sirleaf in 2006. She was the 24th president of Liberia and had the grace to be in power till 2018 and transferred the regalia of power to a new comer in the field of politics, a man I have faith will drive Liberia to much greater heights, Amb. George Weah. An ex-footballer who had his share of glory and I believe he will manufacture more glory to Liberians. Sirleaf has become an icon for democracy and women's rights not only in Africa but across the world. I must mention figures like Ameenah Gurib of Mauritius and Namibia's Saara Kuugongelwa. What the female leaders have done is to try and support fellow women in progressive measures to encourage their participation in governance. This must continue even into the near future. Women must hold hands together and continue to support one another in practically genuine terms with a general goal of increasing their role and influence in how the society is managed. I am sure that the entrance of these positively oriented women will culminate into an overflow of recognition of the strength of women and their commitment to efficient leadership and sustenance in the society.

I wish to close this portion by re-emphasizing on the involvement of the youth in nation building. First, allow me to put certain things right with myself first. I have heard several times of conferences and workshops convened with the mission to "empower" or "to capacity build" the youths. I have serious problems with these terms. Empower? Well. I will have to put myself clear and I will do so coherently. There has been a mention of projects and workshops that claim to empower the youth but when you look at the end result and the imagined transformation in the lives of the youths so empowered you are left wondering. To what direction are the youths empowered and for whom are they empowered? When they claim to 'capacity build' the youths and women through day long seminars and workshops which does not offer a knowledge that is resident and self-sufficient, and for that matter has to be reactivated almost all the time using the same means, then we must ask ourselves the fundamental question as to which direction the youths are being capacity built towards. We must ask which tools and means are utilized in the capacity building process. It has come to a time when we must subject ourselves to the real issues affecting Africa due to the specificity and particularity of the African issues. Having a concoction and blend from all sorts of walk is a mere portrait of lack of ingenuity and soberness. Therefore our generations must be taught on the basis of reality in accordance with the existing demands in the continent while taking advantage of the peculiarity of the different regions in Africa.

The Rise of Tanzania's John Magufuli and Why We want more of Him in Africa...

My attention is turned to the successful story in Africa. Now let me turn my attention for a moment about Tanzania's Commander-in-Chief, Dr. John Pombe Magufuli, I prefer his nickname, "The Bulldozer". Coming to power on the 5th November 2015 is a preface upon which the rest of the exploits are examined. He took over from a regime which had a completely different cup of tea. At least with his. And perhaps a different form of cup, if the tea, could have otherwise remained constant. With only two years in office, he has achieved more than some African heads of states and governments achieved during their misconceived "eternal rule". He began to impress on the very day he was given the mantle and in fact, to date, the social media in Tanzania and across Africa has been constantly more effusive in its praise. He forgot where the country had reached, figuratively stating and began to explore a different fresh route. Magufuli has not brought continuity to Tanzania, but dramatic and significant change. He began to impress just days after his inauguration. I am writing at the second year after taking office. Let me begin o his day one as Mr. President. That day, he made a snap unannounced visit to the Ministry of Finance. Then he pulled funds intended for Independence Day celebrations and redirected them to anti-cholera operations! What? Celebrating independence was not important? No. it was not significant. What relevance would this be when his subjects were prisoners of diseases including cholera and an unending poverty? He has since then cancelled the lavish Independence celebrations to free up funds to fight cholera outbreak. Of course you would agree. Celebrating 54 years of independence when people are dying of diseases such as cholera, which was, at least not a major killer many years before independence is just another joke! But in other countries they celebrate nevertheless, they celebrated it at 53 years and years before. I believe by the time the fifth year is over, there will be a reduction, not on the number of cholera reported deaths, but on number of hospitals without malfunctioning equipment and beds and, believe me, the number of people falling sick to be at the hospital. Now, Tanzania has a new way to celebrate the Independence Day: Through cleaning the streets to improve sanitation. Sensible! War on cholera must be won on the basis of hygiene and medical preparedness. So should African states follow the trajectory of Magufuli, the prospects of Africa, which are well elucidated all over her surface, will be realized and Africa will mutate from the pandemic tortures of poverty to strong economic bloc.

I am not done with health. World Aids Day is significantly celebrated in African and quite a lot of money is set aside by the government and different players to celebrate this day. I will not ask why a day such as Aids Day has to be celebrated when the war against HIV/AIDS is not yet won. No. I will not ask what the infection rate in many African nations is with regard to HIV/AIDS and what proportion of the government's spending is set aside for retroviral drugs and medical care for HIV/AIDS patients. But believe you me that nearly 90 percent of the drugs are either a donation or are acquired through support and the participation of the civil society and foreign governments. But our governments set aside some fat money every year to "celebrate" Aids Day. Ridiculous? Well, it may sound. But to them it is a sensitization celebration! I have no problem with celebrations, but of what relevance is it when a population is so devastated and perennially infected and affected, with little or sometimes no medical care, but still afford to have a day to rejoice over an enemy that has defeated her? What is the celebration about then? Inability to fight against Aids or the joy of not having to spend money for medical care and treatment for HIV patients? I hope someday we will have reasons to celebrate the Aids Day, not because the international community celebrate it, but because we shall have concurred the war against HIV/AIDS and our populations will be completely free from it.

Yet another significant step was downsizing, by more than 90 percent the budget a state dinner that celebrates the opening of parliament. Well, we can say downsizing, but it is more than that, and directed that the money be used for, what I also consider prudent and necessary- buying hospital beds. His surprise visit to the Muhimbili National Hospital was revealing and devastating so to speak. Action had to be taken with an urgency of the tiger, and the man at the top had the responsibility. He began a shake-up of the Tanzania Port Authority, and extended it to the Tanzania Revenue Authority as he launched a tax collection drive. The Commissioner General for TRA was suspended and arrested following unpaid tax of 80 billion Tanzanian shillings at the Dar-es-Salaam Port. Earlier the Prime Minister, Kassim Majaliwa, had put the axe on the feet of five senior TRA officials over the same issue. They too were under arrest and criminal investigations were ensued against them. A systematic effort and passion to fight against the endemic corruption in Tanzania has been corroborated. We can talk about the foreign trip suspensions and the radical cost cutting measures such as reduction of sizes of delegation to international meetings, just to mention one. The good thing is, even the president's own delegation has been reduced and, his foreign trips are kept minimal because he has to serve his people right in their country! Her no cow is sacred to be worshipped. Every sin is judged at the justice table and consequences are bore by the offenders. It does not matter the classification of the victims. Even his own cabinet ministers have been subjected to similar tests. In May 2017, he fired his Minister for Energy and Minerals Sospeter Muhongo for understating exports. In June 2017, businessman James Rugemalira and Harbinder Singh Sethi found themselves in court, facing government prosecutors in court. Both were linked to a major corruption case, the Escrow Scandal in 2014 before he came to power, and surprisingly, ordered probe into mineral exports over the past 19 years.

One thing about The Bulldozer is that over his past service to his country in the various capacities, he is free from corruption. As a minister for public works, he was famous for making surprise visits to road construction sites to uncover unethical thieving activities that robed his country tax payers' sweat. Not many public figures in the African continent have similar track records, and on this there is a general consensus without debate. I am sure that he will delve deeper into the structural issues that have allowed public looting to thrive for so long in his country and that he will continue to enjoy the support of the people of Tanzania, including his team, to sweep Tanzania clean. I hope too that a more systematic approach to handle corruption will be unveiled and that there will be personal accountability by every member of the society. I also believe that he will address the issue of the constitution in a more pragmatic and stylish format and that Tanzania will enjoy a more progressive and democratic constitution in East Africa and Africa as a whole. To date, I can confirm and on this I need no other views, The Bulldozer represents the change Africa needs. He represents the aspirations we hold for a better Africa. He appears, should he continue in this path, to be the solution to a myriad of the bedeviling issues affecting our economy as a continent. Of course some people are skeptics and nothing will change their thoughts. But during chemotherapy, the patient wails and finishes his breathe, but soon afterwards, he rejoices that he is well. Even at birth, it is usual for a mother to wail and cry intensely but after puerperal, she smiles with her new born. On the fight against corruption and mis-governance, if it is genuine and at heart, there are cartels who have to cry, there are lords of impunity who through the intensity of the heat must wail, there are champions of darkness who must weep, but in the end, there will be a common good for every member of the society. I encourage Dr. Magufuli to continue on the same path without looking back. The future hold a better promise under his direction. That said, we may not all agree on the principles of democracy in light with Dr. Magufuli's reign and style. But at some level, I must pose the question, which country in Africa will ever deal with her challenges under the premises of a democracy framed and franchised in first class worlds? And what is the value of democracy in a society which has lost its moral fabric and requires an honest redefinition and transformation? There certainly must be a new way of governing Africa. What Africans have demonstrated reveals that a more proactive approach to governance is indeed required.

The new dawn that is fast falling in Africa must acquire the reception it is entitled in the hearts and minds of the African people. My take is that we need to pull ourselves together. The African blood, from the five continents must embrace Africa and begin to advocate for her total liberty from the oppression of her undeserving and selfish misleaders. Every Africa must acquire the voice to speak against the vices in the society. This is the time I must admit that silence is a capital offence and if an African chooses silence over speech, he must be examined appropriately to determine his African proportion. We must act in ways that help us to address our challenges to avoid beyond-the-century mannerism of subservience at the face of oppression. Our wits must be applied in a manner that generally recognizes that our diversity is an opportunity that spells good fortune for us. We must be ready to toil for much longer times in the battle field to end our self-perpetuated and imposed negativity along tribal lines, ethnic composition and religious affiliations. We must remember that during creation we were made all out of one and on this basis we must hold each other's arms in solidarity. Our appetite for honey must not be consumed by acquiring molted sugar. We have to rich the bee hive and acquire honey through our efforts. The young Africans must be admitted into the arena with rigorous training and education on the subjects of beneficial output to Africa. They must take actions that not only have an immediate impact, but will also determine the future of the continent for decades to come because for Africa to reap the dividends she has longed for, it is up to the youthful generation today to make sure that influence is channeled correctly and directed towards relevant issues that affect not only themselves, but generations after them. This can only be achieved if the youths come together and begin to address the challenges before them as a continent. Unity of the African youth is inevitable. The youth must regain interest in Africa and stop theorizing the occurrences in other continents because based on extant evidence, the youths in the other continents are least interested in Africa. Much of our time should be utilized in discussing issues of our continent and not on western soap operas and movies, foreign football clubs and stars, not because it is a sin to discuss them, but because we have too little time to waste part of it on completely unnecessary topics and discussions.

Moving forward, we must declare the kind of environment we want. An environment where we shall be gripped by the zest and passion not to stop at average but to gain the ultimate perfection in all our dealings as long as excellence remains at close ranges. We must present ourselves as hubs of wealth and resources, which of course we are, not only on materialistic capacities but inherent wisdom and rare knowledge of humanity of the recent age and season. We must join hands in every way to ensure that we deliver on the promises our forefathers held when they declared independence and freedom from servitude and colonial oppression. Our turn to light up the African continent must not be renegotiated on the account of greed and timidity. We have to move forward unanimously and proclaim the glory we have long yearned and dreamt of. We have to demonstrate to the world that we can also be responsible for something, not to present ourselves as weak and directionless entity of people. We have to control ourselves from the appetite of greed and senseless accumulation of wealth at the expense of the majority of us. We must give meaning to every son and daughter of the soil, a valid reason why we came before them, and clearly demonstrate that we were begat well in our time and that we served our purpose, not weakly, but strongly and we surmounted the future problems of our societies.

Institutions must be offered the liberty of service according to their establishing codes and objects. We may not all be of the same view that democracy equals to first, multi-partism, second, having three arms of governments, functions and separation of powers notwithstanding, third, periodic elections and so on. But once we have taken a position that creates different independent arms of governance, we must allow these arms to act and operate under no duress but independently. We have seen how several executives have over-utilized their prerogatives to micro-manage the other arms of government, ripping the judiciary the power to grace over justice and the parliament becoming an extension of the executive, absolutely losing its role in checking the executive. I am of the view that the judiciary in many African states is a prime sector that must now spring up into action and begin to perform its roles without further interference. Yes, the sector that has to come of age and must execute its roles without allegiance of any form to individuals, not even other institutions, except the rule of law, is the judicial system in Africa. Ours is, what appears to be, in many cases, a distinct separation of power, and, as good students, we believe that democracy equals to three arms of governance even if one arm controls the other two tyrannically. For most African nations, it's a pity to say, but the judicial framework has fallen short of the glory of both God and man and the handlers in this corridor of injustice must now be alert. In many African states, the voice of reason is never granted the liberty and the benefit of doubt. Patriots who only crime is to diligently expose details of malfeasance in public offices are constantly arrested and disabled while thieves who have carted resources from generation to generation masquerade daily as free men and boast of the inept judicial mechanisms in place. They paradoxically thrive under anoxic and unjust regimes, but my wonder cannot be overestimated because on every election, the thieves are cleansed through the votes, whether this is an aided process as it always is isn't the issue, my concern rests with the agility with which the African voters are choreographed after it all. They are seen to be lovers of short term prestige offered in droplets by the thieving individuals whose appetite and greed for more is never met. The paradox of it all is that the judicial mechanisms have in most cases become a raping tool that labors to reproduce and rebrand thieves are mere victims of victimization and manslaughter. Whether the courts get a share in doing this I don't know, but there is a sense in which corruption in the judiciary is making the labors of democracy as painful and meaningless as colonization. We need men who can stand tall and with the voice of an optimistic African, condemn, not only condemn, act by reading the riot act, when confronted with implicative cases of open corruption and looting as the cases are always. We need to see the looters of billions locked up in jails after repaying their loots and not the village egg thief sentenced for 20 years in prison! There is a letdown in this sense: that the more the capacity of an individual to steal, the lesser the penalties he attracts from the courts. This must stop so that we redeem ourselves from the negative portrait this practice has given us. We cannot live in a society where our good men are vilified but the robbers are praised and honored by electing them into public offices.

Convincingly, our testaments are juxtaposed in this very significant thought. Until we come to the moment when we identify with our true probes and resolve to tackle them from within, we shall at best only be dealing with the symptoms of our problems, we will never deal with the disease that causes us the problems. We must begin developing and equipping our younger generations as leaders who will serve us in the best of our centric purposes. We have a goal as a society. This must be undertaken without delay. We have to reboot as a continent and begin to move towards the choice direction of economic success and prosperity. This is why I am persuaded that all other pursuits are secondary until we realize the advent of visionary leaders in the continent.

What happens when a public officer in Africa is named in corruption case? Well, I am sure in other parts of the world, one involved in such a case would soon resign without much struggle. Back in this continent, they'd rather die than resign, yet they have stolen everything they were put in-charge of. We must develop a sense of responsibility on public management and administration. Our pursuits to venture into the land of Eldorado is senseless and pointless as long as we continue to love thieves to be in control of our affairs. So we must have in place mechanisms to effectively deal with those who are found to be acting in ways that undermine our commitment and this must be done without prejudice and favor. What matters is delivering quality services to the African people.

When Africa corrects her leadership teething troubles, there is hope that socio-economic prosperity and political sensibility will be the only results. Until now, one must be very weary when you hear of reports by international bodies such as the World Bank and the IMF that try to convince us that our economy is growing. The truth is our economy is degenerating at an alarming speed as a continent. These bodies continues to rely on statistical evidence and formulae to determine growth without assessing the quality of growth. Such reports have been generated for so long but our sorry states have continued to be our greatest challenge. We have read several pages purporting to portray Africa as rising but back on the ground Africans continue to die of hunger and lack of medical care, among other basic human needs. Many African countries have had tremendous increase in their annual budgetary allocations but the question remains, why are we still poorer even with increased budgets? African countries have ministries with roles and objectives but these ministries cannot create jobs and provide a working environment that will accommodate private developers and self-employment in the countries. Public sector has been turned into a casino which benefits the almighty rich lots who can place their bets. It is no longer meant to benefit the people. The society is turned upside down, unplugged from its moral nucleus leading to depletion of hope for a brighter future.

The challenges in Africa have been misdiagnosed and the miseducation of the Africans can be cited to be a great impediment to the progress of the continent. Well, I am of that school but Africa has no shortage of elites complete with full professorial titles in every field. Ironically we cannot feed ourselves, we cannot make our own crop seeds, we cannot treat our sick, we cannot make our own telephones and mobile despite producing the ingredients used in the mobile industry, we cannot build our own roads and bridges, when you take a look, it is the Chinese who are in this industry. We cannot claim to be governing ourselves yet constantly our governments have to be informed and lectured on every dot of good governance. These begs the question, why is Africa faced with all these pitfalls and has to depend on perpetual aid to feed her population despite having holders of doctorate and philosophy in agricultural fields and other associated industries? I tell you for a fact, Africans have been miseducated. Africans have no faith in themselves. Africa is on the receiving end and does not question what she receives. African is intimidated and appears to be a confused continent where thieves are elected into political offices and are expected to guard the resources and preside over the equitable distribution of the same resources they target to pounce on. This continent has borrowed heavily from other continents and today, her identity, originality and authenticity is long lost. It is high time we begun to treat our continent with the respect and honor it deserves. To credit to our continent the real meaning and value of her true self. To caution ourselves from greed and lust of the large, knowing that in this continent, there is sufficiency for man's needs but not his greed. It is what we have to do because we have to be the change which we hope to see in the world.

I invite you to the occasion of unveiling a new Africa. An Africa of merit based leadership and accountability. A place where we all have a right of fair share of belonging and ownership. This is the mental picture we have to create for our generation and pass it on to the next generations without tainting our prospects. We must begin to award the best in our midst, vilify wrong and despicable acts and actors while promoting the just and coherent amongst us. A time for this continent to embrace and value the role of her youthful population has come. Yet this youthful population must grasp with two arms their critical responsibility, role and position in creating a progressive world. We must acknowledge the gains we have made as a people over the past times and begin to look into how best we can cascade some of the unique qualities and achievements we credit to ourselves to the future hopes and development of our nations. This calls upon a mindset that is inwardly transformed and resolute to appropriately underscore the passion and zeal to create a better society.

The re-writing of the African story must begin with us. We must accord this noble task the most of decent time and priority. Let us consolidate our efforts, mental vigor, charisma, zest, passion, longings and all our cravings for the best and the ultimate good of our continent, to the struggle to make Africa the glorious block it was designed, by act of divine creation and choice to be. Let our struggles begin internally by rejecting any temptation to be engulfed in the cloud of selfishness and amnesia, to pursue rightly our goals for the common good of all of us. We must begin rejecting fake leaders who have no visions and call to serve Africa. And this we must do together. A revolution that will sweep away despots and tyrants across Africa must start in African and by the African people themselves. Once we have demonstrated that we can rule and govern ourselves justly, we will earn respect and not be obliged to be part of mediocrity and illegitimate statutes and treaties coaxed on us by other nations. We shall then begin to define our terms and conditions for democracy, justice and the rule of law and order. Until then, our existence on the surface of the earth will invoke despair and regrets but will also be seen as a weakness that must be addressed. The failure to elect leaders of reformed minds and objectives will be used by other civilizations to continue to drive their illicit agendas and interests upon Africa, and subtly, this interaction will leave Africa closer to hell than a sanctuary of new hope and power, as it was designed at the creation.

About the Author

Cavine Onyango Oguta was born and raised in Rachuonyo District in Kenya and educated at St. Douglas Weta Primary school, Kabianga Boys High School and Eldoret University. Currently, he is pursuing his studies at Ghent University, Belgium in the field of Aquaculture. Oguta developed interest in public speaking and writing while at primary school and continued to pursue these interests afterwards. He has been involved in speeches writing and public speech delivery to the young people and in social and political settings. While in primary and secondary school, he composed poems and songs that were meant to influence his audience to think in a particular direction. His literary works were not however published but they were his foundational premises to writing. He has continued with a keen determination to be a writer of inspirational scale, with some level of interests in public governance and development. He has participated in student mentorship programs and coordinated student associations and youth groups. He continues to be a source of inspiration to many young people.

www.ingramcontent.com/pod-product-compliance
Lightning Source LLC
Chambersburg PA
CBHW032030290526
45786CB00011B/1285